CELTIC FC
THE IRELAND
CONNECTION

CELTIC FC

THE IRELAND CONNECTION

BRIAN McGUIRK

BLACK & WHITE PUBLISHING

First published 2009
by Black & White Publishing Ltd
29 Ocean Drive, Edinburgh EH6 6JL

1 3 5 7 9 10 8 6 4 2   09 10 11 12 13

ISBN: 978 1 84502 248 8

Typeset by Ellipsis Books Ltd, Glasgow
Printed and bound by MPG Books Ltd, Bodmin

CONTENTS

ACKNOWLEDGEMENTS

When the idea for this book was hatched I made contact with many people in Ireland, Scotland and Canada. I want to take this opportunity to sincerely thank many of them for their guidance, direction, permission and, of course, their patience.

I would especially like to thank Jim Greenan of the Paul Johnson Celtic Supporters Club in Monaghan Ireland for that initial phone call to me after I had spoken to him about the idea on the ferry to Scotland to see Celtic. Jim advised me to speak to Dr Joseph Bradley and detail my idea to him. The subsequent phone call to Joe proved vital and I thank him for his support, advice, direction and patience throughout this project.

I would also like to acknowledge the use of Dr Bradley's words on sectarianism in the chapter 'The Identity of Celtic' and also David W. Potter for his kind permission to use numerous quotes from his publication *Willie Maley, The Man Who Made Celtic*. I wish too to acknowledge the use of parts from James E. Handley's publication *The Celtic Story – A History of Celtic Football Club* in the chapters 'Brother Walfrid', 'Irish Tricolour and Flag Issue of 1952' and 'Walfrid's Men of Vision'. I would like to acknowledge the use of Michael Kelly's words from the souvenir programme on Brother Walfrid in the chapter 'Brother Walfrid' and wish to thank Michael for kindly agreeing to write the Foreword to this book for me. I would like to acknowledge the use of the words from Daniel McDonagh's poem on Brother Walfrid in the chapter 'Brother Walfrid' and the use of various historical quotes on Celtic from the Kerrydale Street website in the Appendices on 'Players and Staff from Ireland and of Irish Descent', 'Celtic Historical Facts and Supporter Association Facts'.

I would like to thank Conal Duffy of The Rosses Celtic Supporters Club in Donegal for the pleasure of his company at lots of Association of Irish Celtic Supporters Clubs meetings up and down Ireland and for the information received on the sod taken from Donegal and planted in Celtic Park. I would like to acknowledge the use of these words, now on The Rosses Celtic Supporters Club website for the chapter 'Sods from Donegal and Michael Davitt'. I would like to thank Paddy Sweeney from Dungloe Donegal, Secretary of The Association of Donegal Celtic Supporters Clubs for his kind permission to use various historical Celtic facts taken from its website and used in this book. I would like to acknowledge the use of various historical facts on Belfast Celtic taken from The Grand Old Team website on the famous Belfast Celtic. I would like to thank Michael O'Hara from Glasgow, a great grandson of John O'Hara, one of Brother Walfrid's select few who, with him, founded Celtic Football Club in 1887/88, for information received. Michael also pointed me towards Black & White Publishing. Thanks Michael. I would like to thank Tommy Donnelly of the Bamalea Celtic Supporters Club in Ontario, Canada and the Vice President of the North American Federation of Celtic Supporters Clubs, originally from the Gorbals in Glasgow, for his words on the formation history of the Federation used in the Appendices 'Celtic Historical Facts and Supporter Association Facts'.

ACKNOWLEDGEMENTS

I would like to give a special thanks to the Association of Irish Celtic Supporters Clubs (AICSC) and to Philip Fitzpatrick, the official photographer to the AICSC from Co. Monaghan, Ireland, for their kind permission to use numerous photographs in this publication. For anyone else who has permitted me to use photographs received and used in this book, thank you so much.

For anyone I have missed out, your contribution to this book is spiritually acknowledged: thank you all.

And finally, but maybe most importantly, I would like to thank my wife Ann and my children Brian and Sinead for listening to me over the years going on constantly about Celtic and travelling to Glasgow to see them play, and saying that I was going to write a book on it. I have now.

Brian McGuirk

FOREWORD

There has always been a great well of support and goodwill for Celtic in Ireland. Indeed, how could it be any other way? We all, as the song says, 'know the history'. What country in the world could be at the forefront of such an institution in world football and fail to be proud of its creation?

The account of Irish men and women being driven from their homeland through hunger, poverty and other such by-products of a foreign occupation and proceeding to rise again and make great contributions to their adopted homelands is one that can be, and has been, told many times over.

In the same way, the story of Brother Walfrid and the club he established to raise funds to feed the immigrant Irish youngsters and which went on to conquer Europe captured the imagination of many Irish. In particular, a deep affection for the club was passed down from generation to generation by those Irish and their offspring who have lived and worked in the West of Scotland and followed the Celts.

The strong links forged by Walfrid and his colleagues between Ireland and Celtic endure to this very day thanks to a strong supporter base that ensures that these traditions are passed down from generation to generation in story and in song.

Today, modern multimedia, enhanced transport links between Scotland and Ireland and a well-organised and motivated network of supporters clubs keep the connection vibrant and ensure that the torch can be passed on to the younger generation. Indeed, with many Irish players now featuring in the first team and through the ranks of the reserve and youth set-ups, it could be argued that the Celtic-Ireland love affair is as lively as ever.

Celtic is more than just a club and, as long as it has its history and as long as there are supporters around to ensure that the flame lit by Walfrid endures, it will remain that way.

Hail, hail!

Michael Kelly

Secretary, Association of Irish Celtic Supporters Clubs

INTRODUCTION

The idea for this book came about from a phone call I received from Gerry McDonnell of the Michael Dwyers Celtic Supporters Club in County Wicklow a few years back. At the time we were both active members within the Association of Irish Celtic Supporters Clubs. Gerry is the Assistant Chairman (at the time of writing) and I was the Leinster Representative of the Association and the Chairman of the Dún Dealgan Celtic Supporters Club at the time. Gerry had called me about a statement printed in an Irish newspaper written by a sports journalist writing for the *Wicklow People,* a newspaper in southeast Ireland. While writing an article on Celtic the journalist asked the question 'why do people in Ireland support a team that plays its football in Scotland?' Surely this question is rhetorical? This question is something that Celtic supporters in Ireland are taunted with every day. There are many reasons why Irish people and our diaspora support Celtic. The topics written about in this book identify these reasons and are based on historical facts; facts that join Celtic supporters in Ireland to our diaspora in Scotland and indeed worldwide.

Celtic Football Club will remain forever conscious and proud of its Irish roots. But for the supporters of this great club this book has been written to state unequivocally 'This is why we support Celtic'. Much has been written about Celtic over the years but nothing has been written that clearly sets out why

xiii

Irish people and the diaspora worldwide support Celtic. There is one reason why we all do – 'We do know our history'.

This book *Celtic FC – The Ireland Connection* brings together a range of material to emphasise the Irish connection and identity of Celtic and its worldwide support. In recent years there has been a real reawakening of Celtic and its identity with Ireland. It's the identity and connection to Ireland that makes this so different from other published work. This is Celtic's story from Ireland's perspective.

Celtic is a club that we Irish and our diaspora can proudly call our own. Celtic as a club is unique in this respect. If you are Irish, or of Irish descent, then Celtic is a part of your heritage. Celtic is our legacy, left to us by the courage and vision of Irish men like Brother Walfrid, John Glass and Pat Welsh, to name but a few. Many of the 'great men' involved in Celtic's formation were immigrants into Glasgow from their native Ireland, a country crippled by famine and political unrest.

We didn't just happen to support Celtic; Celtic is a part of us. Celtic for us is so much more than a football club. Celtic is an institution, an identity and a celebration of being Irish or being of Ireland. Celtic is a legacy passed from generation to generation. Celtic is a way of life.

When our forefathers left Ireland and took the boat to Scotland in search of a better life, they did so not knowing what lay in store. They left a country in the midst of famine and political unrest only to enter into the same desperation in Scotland. The Irish in Glasgow at the time, living in the squalor of the east end, needed a guiding figure, someone or something to give meaning to their existence, while never forgetting their roots.

INTRODUCTION

One of the resultant effects of the Famine (1845–51) was the displacement of two million Irish to seek respite elsewhere. Many travelled to Glasgow where work in this industrial city would provide for them and their families what they had lacked in Ireland. Sanctuary was not altogether forthcoming and they found themselves confined mostly to the slums of the east end, scraping an existence as they had in Ireland.

In the beginning, Celtic provided money to assist the immigrant Irish in Glasgow's east end and became a symbol for Irish Catholics in the West of Scotland. It helped give a displaced community a sense of being, a belonging amidst deprivation and hostility.

This book is a journey through the history of Ireland and that of Celtic that bears direct links to Ireland. It is the story of Famine in Ireland, emigration to Scotland and the founding of Celtic by a displaced people. The founding of a football club that gave the then Irish community a sense of being amid adversity and that today gives a diaspora throughout the world an identity and a link to Ireland.

1

THE FAMINE

Ireland is in your hands, in your power. If you do not save
her, she cannot save herself. I solemnly call upon you to recol-
lect that I predict with the sincerest conviction that a quarter
of her population will perish unless you come to her relief.

Daniel O'Connell to the British House of Commons, 1847.

Prior to the Great Famine (*An Gorta Mór* 1845–1851) the Irish
had suffered famine several times. 'Scorched earth warfare',
as practised by the warring parties in the Desmond Rebellions,
had caused a devastating famine in Munster and bad harvests
caused by extremely bad weather conditions in 1741 resulted
in the starvation of nearly a quarter of a million people in
what is generally considered the first Irish Famine.

In 1798 there was a countrywide rebellion against British
rule. The rebellion failed and as a result many Irish were
hanged or tortured. The English Army was increased to nearly
100,000 men to thwart any future uprisings.

Two years later, in 1800, the Act of Union was made law
and it made Ireland a part of the United Kingdom. The Act
abolished the 500–year-old independent Irish Parliament in

Dublin and placed the country under the jurisdiction of Britain's Parliament at Westminster, England. Although Ireland was to be represented there by 100 members, Catholics were excluded.

The Penal Laws were imposed in Ireland in 1695 to punish the Irish for supporting the Catholic Stewart King, James II, in his battle to ascend the British throne in place of the Protestant, William of Orange. The Penal Laws were meant as a tool to push the Irish into submission and were justified by the British Government as necessary to retain the character of the Irish.[1]

With an Irish Catholic army at his side, James II had been defeated at the Battle of the Boyne in July 1690. The resulting Penal Laws stripped Irish Catholics of their rights including: the ability to serve as an officer in the British Army or Navy; hold any government office; vote; buy land; practise law; attend school; serve an apprenticeship; possess weapons and practise their religion. The Catholic Church was outlawed. The Gaelic language was banned. Export trade was forbidden as Irish commerce and industry were deliberately destroyed.

With eighty per cent of Ireland being Catholic, the Penal Laws were intended to degrade the Irish so severely that they would never again be in a position to seriously threaten Protestant rule. In 1600 Protestants had owned just ten per cent of Ireland's land. By 1778, Protestants owned ninety-five per cent of the land. When a Catholic landowner died, the estate was divided up equally among all of his sons, diluting the value. However, if any son renounced Catholicism and became a Protestant, he automatically inherited all of his father's property.

THE FAMINE

Catholic emancipation occurred in 1829, largely through the efforts of Daniel O'Connell, a brilliant Catholic lawyer who lived in Derrynane, County Kerry. Daniel O'Connell was born on 6 August 1775 in Carhen, near Caherciveen, County Kerry, to a once-wealthy Roman Catholic family. Under the patronage of his wealthy bachelor uncle, Maurice 'Hunting Cap' O'Connell, he studied at Douai in France. In his early years he became acquainted with the pro-democracy radicals of the time and committed himself to bringing equal rights and religious tolerance to his own country. But by now Ireland was a country subdued.

With the end of the French Revolution in 1789, Napoleon Bonaparte attempted to conquer Europe. The Napoleonic Wars began in 1802 with Europe and her allies forming an alliance to fight against Napoleon and his armies. Britain joined the battle in 1803 fighting Napoleon on all fronts. Napoleon was eventually defeated and exiled. With the end of the Napoleonic Wars in 1815, British soldiers retuned home, leading to increased unemployment. Furthermore, as Europe transitioned from war to peace, a depression began and the Irish economy began to falter. Britain turned its attention from Europe and refocused its attention on its colonial holdings. The economic goal of British colonialism was to extract the greatest amount of resources and exports from the source to the benefit of the British landowners.

By the mid- 1800s, English politicians thought that Ireland was a country in need of change. The old Irish traditions needed to be changed and Ireland needed to be brought into the English assumption of the modern world. To the industrious, ambitious British, their rural Irish neighbours seemed to be an alien, rebellious, backward people, stuck in an ancient past and they hoped to remake the Irish in their own image.

From 1816 onward, wet weather destroyed crops, the potato failed in several provinces and, weakened by hunger, more than 100,000 Irish died of starvation and disease.

Ireland's population doubled during this period to over eight million. Good potato crops meant the people were generally well fed but there were very few employment opportunities. The Act of Union had resulted in Ireland's economy being absorbed by Britain. Although free trade now existed between the two countries, England generally used Ireland as a dumping ground for its surplus goods. Rapid industrialisation in Britain also brought the collapse of the Irish linen and woollen industries in the countryside with their less efficient handlooms. The British 'Poor Enquiry' survey conducted in 1835 revealed that seventy-five per cent of Irish labourers were without any regular work and that begging was common.

The British government enacted the Poor Law Act of 1838, modelled on the English workhouse system. Under this relief plan, Ireland was divided into 130 separate administrative areas, called unions, since they united several church parishes together. Each union had its own workhouse and a local Board of Guardians elected by taxpaying landowners and farmers. The chairman of the board was usually the biggest proprietor or landlord in the area. Each board was responsible for setting local tax rates and for collecting the funds necessary to maintain the workhouse. Inside each workhouse lived a resident Master and Matron, who were also supervised by the board. The entire system was supervised by a Poor Law Commissioner stationed in Dublin.[2]

THE FAMINE

In the fifty years preceding the famine up to 200 commissions and special committees were instructed to report on the state of Ireland and without exception their findings prophesied disaster: yet still nothing was done to prevent disaster occurring. Ireland was on the verge of starvation, her population was rapidly rising, three quarters of her labourers were unemployed and housing conditions were appalling. The British government ignored all these reports and instead introduced, in July 1838, the Irish Poor Law Act which stated that the property of Ireland must support the poverty of Ireland and the menace to Britain be removed. In other words, Ireland must fend for herself.

Most housing conditions in British owned and administrated Ireland were wretched. The census in 1841 graded 'houses' in Ireland into four classes; the fourth and lowest class consisted of windowless mud cabins of a single room, in which nearly half of the rural population of Ireland lived. Furniture was a luxury; the inhabitants of a town land in Donegal numbering about 9,000 people had, in 1837, only ten beds, ninety-three chairs and 243 stools between them. The evicted and unemployed put roofs over ditches burrowed into banks in fields and existed in bog holes. By 1841, when a census was taken, the population had reached 8,175,124, but when the famine came in 1845 the population might well have been above ten million.[3]

Meanwhile, in 1844, a report was received that in North America a disease, hitherto unknown, had attacked the potato crop. In August 1845 Sir Robert Peel, the British Prime Minister, received a letter from the Isle of Wight reporting that the disease had appeared in the potato crop there and was spreading throughout England. It was now only a question of time before the blight spread to Ireland. In October it was time for the potatoes to be taken out of the ground. The soundness of the potato when first dug was responsible for bewildering contradictions. Within a few days the fine-looking tubers had become a stinking mass of corruption and they all rotted. Alarm turned to terror and the standard of living plummeted.

In Ireland, on the eve of the Famine, the spirit of rebellion had once again arisen. Led by the brilliant orator, Daniel O'Connell, growing numbers of Irish were demanding self-government for Ireland through repeal of the Act of Union. The Repeal Movement featured mass rallies filled with O'Connell's fiery oratory. At one such rally in County Meath, nearly 750,000 persons came together on the Hill of Tara, a former seat of the High Kings of Ireland.

The Repeal Movement peaked in October 1843 as Daniel O'Connell and half a million supporters attempted to gather near Dublin for another 'monster' rally, but this time they encountered British cannons, warships and troops ready for a violent confrontation. To avoid a potential massacre, O'Connell ordered his people to disperse. The British arrested the sixty-eight-year-old O'Connell. While in prison his health broke and his Repeal Movement faded. He died just a few years later on 15 May 1847, leaving Ireland leaderless and without a charismatic voice during its darkest period.

From a humanitarian point of view every famine, regardless of its cause, development and aftermath, is a terrible disaster. In retrospect, however, the Great Famine has seemingly constructed itself over the course of centuries. Aided by over-population, poverty and a food supply depending on one crop, the process gained momentum at the end of the eighteenth century. Warnings from scientists and, from the mid 1800s onwards, from nature, were neglected and in September 1845 the house of cards collapsed.

Almost overnight about half of the potato crops in Ireland had become inedible by the plant disease blight. The loss of this food supply could not be absorbed by a society which had been weakened by a complex accumulation of demographic, economic and agricultural developments. Ireland was plunged into the blackest period of its history: the Great Famine, or *An Gorta Mór*.

At the beginning of the year 1845 the state of Ireland was, as it had been for nearly 700 years, a source of grave anxiety to Britain. Ireland had first been invaded in 1169 by the Normans, and yet by 1845 it was neither assimilated nor subdued. The country had been conquered not once but several times, the population had been brought to the verge of extinction, but an Irish nation still existed, separate and hostile.

The land of Ireland was owned by British landlords, many of whom controlled vast estates of over 50,000 acres each. All the landlords lived in big houses or castles, but some of them lived in Britain and never saw their estates, which were managed by agents who collected the rents from the tenants.

All the wretchedness and misery could almost, without exception, be traced to a single source – the system under which land had come to be occupied and owned in Ireland; a system produced by centuries of successful conquests, rebellions, confiscations and punitive legislation. These were the principal causes of Irish misery and the poor relations between landlords and tenant.

When potatoes were being cultivated, 2,385,000 persons were without employment. Unless an Irish labourer could get hold of a patch of land and grow potatoes on which to feed himself and his children, the family starved. The land was divided and sub-divided again and again, and holdings were split into smaller and still smaller fragments until families were attempting to exist on plots of less than half an acre. As the population increased and the demand for a portion of ground grew more frantic, land became like gold dust in Ireland. The possession of a piece of land became the difference between life and death, and, as a result, the rents in Ireland were enormous.

During the summer of 1845, blight devastated Ireland's potato crop, the staple food in the Irish diet. When the potatoes were dug from the ground, they turned into slimy, decaying handfuls of rot. 'Famine fever' – cholera, dysentery, scurvy, typhus and infestations of lice soon spread throughout the Irish countryside. Skeletal children cried with pain, their features sharpened with hunger and their limbs wasted so that there was little left but bones. The dead were buried in mass graves, often only a few inches below ground. Over the next decade, more than one million Irish men, women and children died and another two million left their homeland for Britain, Canada and the United States. Within five years, the Irish population was reduced by a quarter.

By October 1845, news of the blight had reached London. British Prime Minister, Sir Robert Peel, quickly established a Scientific Commission to examine the problem. After briefly studying the situation, the Commission issued a gloomy report that over half of Ireland's potato crop might perish due to 'wet rot'.

THE FAMINE

The inadequacy of relief efforts by the British government worsened the horrors of famine. Initially, Britain believed that the free market would end the Famine. In 1846, in a victory for advocates of free trade, Britain repealed the Corn Laws, which protected domestic grain producers from foreign competition. The repeal of the Corn Laws failed to end the crisis since the Irish lacked sufficient money to purchase foreign grain.

In the spring of 1847, Britain adopted other measures to cope with famine, setting up soup kitchens and programmes of emergency work relief, but many of these programmes ended when a banking crisis hit Britain. In the end, Britain relied largely on a system of workhouses, which had originally been established in 1838. But these grim institutions had never been intended to deal with a crisis of such sweeping scope. Some 2.6 million Irish entered overcrowded workhouses, where more than 200,000 died.

The blight attacked not only the crops in the field but also the crops in storage during mild and damp periods. In 1845, blight destroyed forty per cent of Irish potatoes and the following year almost the entire crop was ruined. The subsequent 'Black 47' yielded the same increases in famine, emigration and disease. Although there were no crop failures from 1847–1851, famine conditions intensified due to the lack of seed potatoes for planting new crops and often inadequate planting for fear blight would strike again.

Tenant farmers held short-term leases which were payable each six months in arrears. If they failed to pay the rent due they were jailed or evicted and their homes burned. During 1845–1847, some 500,000 people were evicted, many of whom died of starvation or entered the badly run poorhouses that existed.[4] The only other option available was emigration. From 1845–1855 more than two million people emigrated. In 1851, a quarter of a million left Ireland for overseas destinations. They tended to go to Britain, the United States, Canada, New Zealand and Australia. Britain was reluctant to provide assistance to the inferior people of Ireland, as they viewed them. The government officials supported a policy of non-intervention, which maintained the belief that it was counterproductive to interfere in economics. The chief instrument of relief came in the form of low-paid work projects to promote industrialisation and modernise Ireland. Robert Peel repealed the Corn Laws, enabling the Irish to import grain from North America. This action saw him deposed as Prime Minister and replaced by John Russell, who was less lenient on the Irish. Relief measures, such as corn importation, were sent from North America; however, these shipments were mere tokens to the necessary relief required to comfort the starving.[5]

In 1847 the public works projects were abandoned by the government and instead poorhouses were established by private groups, such as the church and Quakers. During the entire Famine period, 173 workhouses were built throughout Ireland. The workhouses themselves were not in a condition to become centres of relief. In the parts of Ireland which were now most distressed, the workhouses, from the day they opened, had been insolvent, dirty and disorganised. Several were on the point of closing their doors. Scarriff, in Clare, was about to shut, and at Clifden in Galway the workhouse had actually been closed and the destitute expelled. The soup kitchens were very welcome and each person received a bowl of soup and some bread. According to Charles Trevelyan, the crisis was over in 1847, whereupon all emergency relief came to a standstill. This would turn out to be the worst year of the Great Famine.

The Irish relief effort was put under the control of the thirty-eight-year-old English civil servant Charles Edward Trevelyan, Assistant Secretary of the British Treasury. Trevelyan was appointed by Prime Minister Peel to oversee relief operations in Ireland and would become the single most important British administrator during the Famine years. He was a brilliant young man of unimpeachable integrity but was also stubborn, self-righteous, overly bureaucratic and not given to a favourable opinion of the Irish. He handled all the day-to-day duties himself, unwilling to delegate any of his responsibilities so that, inevitably, important decisions were often put on hold or never addressed at all.

Trevelyan would visit Ireland just once during all of the famine years, venturing only as far as Dublin, far from the hard-hit west of Ireland. Remoteness from the suffering, he once stated, kept his judgment more acute than that of his administrators actually working among the people affected. For his work as administrator of relief to famine stricken Ireland from 1845–1847 he was named a KCB.

The contemporary comment that God sent the blight but that the British made the Famine is perhaps more appropriate. Although the words are different, the meaning of the words written by the British Prime Minister Tony Blair in 1997 is the same:

The Famine was a defining event in the history of Ireland and of Britain. It has left deep scars. That one million people should have died in what was then part of the richest and most powerful nation in the world is something that still causes pain as we reflect on it today. Those who governed in London at the time failed their people through standing by while a crop failure turned into a massive human tragedy. We must not forget such a dreadful event.

In the aftermath of the Famine typhus fever and other diseases began to ravage Ireland. The main epidemic in 1847 was typhus and relapsing fever but at the same time other diseases afflicted starving Ireland. Dysentery, famine dropsy, diarrhoea and scurvy were horrible diseases which affected many people, resulting in agonising death. The courage of those who came to the help of the people is beyond praise. Doctors, Catholic priests, medical staff officials and many others all contracted fever and died. The workhouses, fever hospitals and dispensaries did valuable work. Conditions in workhouses were dreadful. Fever patients lay naked on straw, the living and the dead together. There was little medicine, little drink and few medical staff. In workhouses and fever hospitals, the epidemic seems to have reached its height in April, when, during a single week, thousands of inmates of workhouses were officially reported to have died.

In September 1847 the epidemic began to subside when the number of people infected began to decline. In many districts, however, the epidemic continued even into the following year. The total of those who died during the fever epidemic and of famine diseases will never be known, but probably ten times more died of disease than of starvation. The corpses were buried in fields, hillsides and ditches unknown to anyone. In lonely districts fever-stricken persons died in their cabins without anyone coming near them and their bodies were left to rot. In Clifden, County Galway, corpses were burned and in other districts they were buried under the cabin floor. Too many had died for funeral services to be held.

As the famine and fever intensified, the minds of the Irish people turned to emigration. In a great mass movement, they made their way to America and Britain. They left Ireland with hatred in their hearts for the British government. Historians estimate that more than a million emigrated from Ireland to North America and about the same to Britain. Many also emigrated to Canada because the fares were low or the landlords paid their way, before crossing the border into America at the first opportunity.

They were unwelcome in America because they were destitute and they were carrying fever. They sheltered in cellars, basements of houses and derelict houses until they found proper housing. When they secured work they sent money home for their relatives to join them, but it was not until the second or third generation of immigrants that the Irish began to establish themselves and become successful and powerful in the country of their adoption.

The Irish in overwhelming masses crossed the Irish Channel to land at ports in England, Scotland and Wales. This was the flight of the very poor that did not have the money for the fare to America or Canada. There was an irresistible attraction to Britain, as the starving were given food and would not be allowed to die of hunger. Thousands of men, women and children were on the roads, moving towards the coast, most of them begging their way. The main ports of arrival were Liverpool, Glasgow, Swansea, Cardiff and Newport.

In January 1847, the number of destitute Irish arriving became a deluge. In the spring of 1847 tens of thousands of feverish destitute Irish spread over England, Scotland and Wales, moving on from the ports, afraid of being sent back to Ireland. Not only were the Irish disliked, any hope that the misery of the destitute might evoke compassion was destroyed by fear of fever. The doors of the charitable were closed against them. The majority never escaped from destitution, but wandered around the country existing on charity and outdoor relief.

By the middle of 1847 the soup kitchens had extended to every part of Ireland. Upwards of three million people were fed every day in the neighbourhood of their own homes. The harvest in September was promising but the acreage was low, because of the lack of seed, and the labour was not there to cultivate the land.

The British government considered that its responsibility towards the starving Irish was almost at an end. The Irish Poor Law Extension Bill legalising outdoor relief and transferring the destitute to the Irish Poor Law and the Irish Poor Rates became law on 8 June 1847. On 15 August the phasing out of the soup kitchens commenced, and by October everything was closed. Trevelyan instructed that all operations were to be wound up.

At the end of 1847 Britain had a major financial crisis and there was no money available for Ireland. The Irish Poor Law Rates were impossible to collect because the landlords would not pay up. In the first week of October 1847 Trevelyan stayed for a few days in Dublin to confer with his officials. It was his first visit to Ireland since the Famine began. The workhouses were in dire financial straits and did not have the money for food for the occupants.

Many letters of appeal from officials and the most responsible people in Ireland were received in London, all pointing out the desperate situation, but Charles Wood, Trevelyan and Lord John Russell were not to be moved. Lord Clarendon made an urgent appeal to Lord John Russell that the people must not be allowed to die of starvation. Some workhouses had collapsed. Clifden in Galway was bankrupt, it had closed down and the wretched inmates had been expelled. By the middle of December the number of destitute, half-naked and starving, who were besieging the workhouses made it evident that outdoor poor relief must be renewed immediately.

The Lord-Lieutenant of Ireland warned the government that insurrection in Ireland was at hand. Landlords, their agents and hostile officials were being shot daily and many of their attackers were escaping to England. The government introduced a Bill in the House of Commons called the Crime and Outrage (Ireland) Bill on 29 November, and three bodies of 5,000 men each were sent to Arklow, Clonmel and Limerick City. The Repeal Association was the mouthpiece and champion of the Irish masses, with branches in every town and village and repeals wardens and repeal police in every parish.

In the spring of 1848 potatoes were planted all over Ireland and hopes were high that the Famine was over. But from the middle of June 1848, the terrible story of 1846 was repeated blow after blow and by the middle of July the catastrophe had begun. Even before the crushing blow of the new potato

15

failure, the condition of the people was worse than in the previous year. Lord John Russell, Sir Charles Wood and Trevelyan would not advance any more money for Ireland, and all the officials were ordered to return home. On 1 July the funds of the British Association were exhausted and the 200,000 children that were being fed were now left to die.

A wave of alarm swept over the country and everyone who could scrape the money together prepared to leave Ireland. A new emigration began. The emigration of 1848 was very different from the disorganised flight of 1847. A thousand a week were leaving and comfortable farmers from Meath and Westmeath were said to be arriving in Dublin daily by the hundreds. In Mayo thousands of acres were left without a single inhabitant or animal and in Munster large tracts of arable land were either deserted or squatted on by paupers. Substantial towns were becoming deserted and all the respectable sections of the population were leaving. Meanwhile, the wretched hordes of destitute were being treated with increasing harshness. Thousands were descending on the workhouses screaming for food only to be turned away.

On 27 December 1848, Lord Clarendon wrote to Trevelyan in despair. The first few months of 1849 saw as much destitution, if not more, than at any time since the potato failed. Jails had already become a refuge and men had committed crimes to be transported out of Ireland. The Chief Poor Law Commissioner resigned because he would not agree with a policy of extermination. Ireland lost her last remaining friend, for in June 1849 the Quakers gave up relief work. The number of people in workhouses had risen to 250,000 and the number on outdoor relief had risen to 770,000. Horrifying reports of the state of the destitute in workhouses came in. The inmates were half-naked and were given just enough food to avoid starvation. In spite of all this the British government remained adamant and refused all requests for relief. The poverty of the Irish people continued, dependence on the potato continued. The treatment of the Irish people by the British government during the famine has been described by some as an act of genocide.

It will never be known how many people died during the Famine and historians often come up with different figures. Before the Famine the unofficial population was almost ten million. But in 1851, after the Famine, it had dropped to six and a half million. It is safe to say that one million died of starvation and two million emigrated to America and Britain. Other famines followed as other famines had gone before, but it is the terrible years of the Great Famine of 1845–1851 that are remembered most.[6]

The Famine of 1845–1851 is often regarded by historians as the worst natural and political disaster ever to afflict Ireland. But, what did occur in Ireland during those terrible years brought together a group of people in the east end of Glasgow; people who had left Ireland in despair and who sought to find a reprieve for their starving countrymen and women in their adopted home. Courageous men, who faced adversity and won, for, without the Famine in Ireland there would surely be no Celtic Football Club today.

2

BROTHER WALFRID

Described by Willie Maley as 'The most enthusiastic Celt of all', Brother Walfrid left behind a legacy that reaches far beyond that of helping to found a football club. His organisational powers enabled him to surround himself with the sort of people whose ideals and principles were instrumental in the founding and survival of Celtic Football Club. Men like John Glass, James Grant, John O'Hara, Joseph Shaughnessy, Dr John Conway, Pat Welsh, William McKillop, James Quillan, Hugh and Arthur Murphy to name but a few great men.

Together, with Walfrid at the helm, the foundations of Celtic were set, foundations that would ensure a place for Celtic on the world stage, a club both envied and adored. He never held an official position of power within the club structure but his influence was immense and extended into every committee and meeting in those early days.

The football game known as soccer was beginning in the latter years of the nineteenth century to hold a fascination for the ordinary working man who was prepared to pay for watching exponents of the sport at play. Soccer provided a release for the newly acquired leisure time. It was not until the 1870s that it became customary for work to cease at one o'clock on Saturdays. Previously on that day work ended at six o'clock and during the week at seven or eight with shops not putting down their shutters until eleven.

The Catholic parish in those days was a self-contained unit. Teachers played a role in its work and leisure activities. A strong link existed that bound school to church. The esteem they created for themselves by their unselfish co-operation with all that was worthy made them exemplars for the men and women of the community. Authority grew with service and their word was law in many a household.

At a time when no official assistance was provided to the underprivileged, the charity provided by the teachers of the Catholic parishes was at its most prevalent. For those who have existed during the time of the Welfare State it is hard to appreciate the narrow line that existed between subsistence and destitution in Victorian times. When the father of a young family lost his job, even temporarily, whether skilled or unskilled, the results were devastating – there was no income for the household. Unemployment benefit was then unknown and as for overtime this entailed the normal working hours so there was little or no chance to save. During the half-century from 1850 to 1900 an adult male labourer's earnings per week of fifty-one hours varied between twelve shillings and twenty-two shillings. In such circumstances parents welcomed the opportunity of a warm meal for the children. To preserve the self-respect of parents a penny was charged for these meals, hence the 'penny dinner' tables. The local branch of the St Vincent de Paul Society in Glasgow's east end co-operated in the good work being done. Expenses were met from church collections, subscriptions and charity concerts.[7]

The man we know as Brother Walfrid was born Andrew Kerins on 18 May 1840 in the village of Ballymote in County Sligo to parents John and Elizabeth.

Ballymote was back then a small village in the barony of Corran in southern Sligo. The main industry was weaving which at its peak employed some three hundred people.[8]

Although little is known of the young Andrew, it is safe to ascertain that the effects of the Famine on the Irish people must have affected him and his desire to 'do good' when he later realised his destiny in life. Sligo, along with north Roscommon, endured the worst of the famine. Andrew was a young lad of five when the first reports of potato blight were recorded in Mayo on 13 September 1845. It is not documented how the Kerins endured the tragedy but, being of farming stock, it is likely that they would not have been left untouched.

In 1855, aged just fifteen, Andrew Kerins, escaping the ravages of famine, took a coal boat to Glasgow in search of work. In Glasgow the Marists had been at the forefront of bringing education and care to the malnourished and poverty-stricken Irish in the east end of the city. Andrew attended night classes provided by the Marist teaching order and his experiences must have been greatly stirred as on 11 September 1864, aged twenty-four, he decided his vocation was to join them. To fulfil this he went to France to continue his religious and professional training at the Marist Novitiate House at Beauchamps.

The Marist teaching order was introduced to Ireland in 1862 with its first house in Sligo.

BROTHER WALFRID

Andrew Kerins adopted the name 'Walfrid' in line with the practice of rejecting worldly ties and assuming a saintly name. He called himself after an Italian citizen of Pisa in the eighth century called Galfrido Della Guerardesca, who was canonised Saint Walfrid.

The Marist Brothers have worked in Scotland since 1838. They were founded in France in January 1817, by Marcellin Champagnat, a young French priest who, after only six months in his first parish, was called to the deathbed of a fifteen-year-old boy. He found the boy to be totally ignorant of God or God's love for him. Realising that this was the situation of most of the youngsters in his parish, Marcellin immediately founded the Marist Brothers. He saw education as the best way of bringing to children the message of God's love for them, and so the conduct of schools became the chief apostolate of the Marist Brothers.

The Marist Brothers came to Glasgow in 1858 and started the St Mungo's Academy. Over the years primary schools followed, St Mungo's in Townhead, St Patrick's in Anderston, St Mary's and St Alphonsus in Calton and the Sacred Heart in Bridgeton. Schools were also opened in Dumfries, Dundee, Wolverhampton, Jarrow and throughout Ireland.

It seemed throughout his training that Brother Walfrid's heart's desire was to return to Glasgow and to the east end in particular. In 1868 he fulfilled this ambition by taking up a teaching post at St Mary's Parochial School in Calton.

The Glasgow Walfrid witnessed upon his return in 1868 was not unlike what he had left behind in Ballymote in 1855. Glasgow, the most densely populated city in Europe at the time, was a scene of squalor, deprivation, poverty, decay, disease and human suffering. Of the 11,675 registered deaths in Glasgow in 1888, 4,750 were children under the age of five. Brother Walfrid seized upon this environment like a man possessed. The Irish children caught up in this turmoil were his prime concern. His parents could never have imagined the journey their son was about to embark upon.

At this time, Walfrid was teaching in St Mary's. The City of Glasgow Bank had failed and, as a direct consequence, the Forge Steelworks was forced to let many workers go, many of them Irish. In the Victorian era the father was the only breadwinner and with so many men out of work the family unit was suffering. The already deprived east end fell further into despair. Children, if they did attend school, were unable to focus because of hunger. In 1874, Walfrid became headmaster of the newly opened Sacred Heart School in the new parish of Sacred Heart, which was carved out of St Mary's parish. Here he gave much assistance to Father Noonan, whose task it was to look after the aspiring Brother Walfrid. Brother Walfrid took over empty premises near the school and began the 'penny dinners' with the financial backing of the local conference of the St Vincent de Paul Society. In addition to encouraging some of the Catholic teams in existence to play charity games for the benefit of his school's dinner table and clothing scheme, he formed football teams among the young men of the parish and prepared a football ground where admission was charged. After building up a number of teams, none of whom existed for long, he devised a set of rules and opened a subscription list for a football team that he proposed to form and call after the land that bore them, 'Celtic Football Club'. Archbishop Eyre, who despite knowing nothing about football was fully prepared to back any project that had for its benefit the members of his poor flock, headed the list. The list was representative of the Catholic Irish in Glasgow.

The Catholic schools in the east end of Glasgow secured for a time a lucrative means to support this charitable work. Football teams had not yet developed into financial companies intent on financing their own interests. However, because of the fervour of their supporters, clubs were induced into playing the occasional game for the work of charity. In the Scottish Capital, Edinburgh Hibernian was formed in 1872 by Irish immigrants to the city under the guidance of Canon Edward Hannon who would occasionally play games for the east end effort and Irish causes elsewhere. Despite Walfrid's scant knowledge of football, he was aware of its growing popularity within the working class of Britain's industrial cities. When Hibernian won the Scottish cup in 1887 the celebrations carried on in St Mary's Hall, East Rose Street (now Forbes Street) in the Calton district of Glasgow. Representatives of St Mary's, St Andrew's and St Alphonsus' parishes met and decided that the time was right for Glasgow to have an Irish football club. During several meetings in 1887, some of them stormy, the groundwork was done. On 6 November 1887 with John Glass presiding as chairman, Glasgow Celtic Football Club was formed. Walfrid's proposal for a football team was accepted and many names were suggested including Glasgow Hibernian, Glasgow Emerald and Emerald Harp, however Brother Walfrid insisted on using the name 'Celtic' (or Keltic as was Walfrid's preferred pronunciation). Walfrid stubbornly held out for the name 'Celtic' against a strong opposition. Under the guidance of Walfrid and men such as

John Glass, Pat Welsh, William McKillop and John Quillan, the newly established club would progress at a rapid pace.

Soon after its inception a circular was issued declaring that the main object of the club was to supply the east-end conferences of the St Vincent de Paul Society with funds for the maintenance of the dinner tables for the needy children in the missions of St Mary's, Sacred Heart and St Michael's.

One week after the founding meeting a six-acre site was leased on 13 November next to Janefield cemetery at a rent of £50 per annum and over the next six months a throng of Irish volunteers and a handful of craftsmen worked day and night to form the first Celtic Park. By the end of November the *Scottish Umpire* would write:

> We learn that the efforts which have lately been made to organise in Glasgow a first-class Catholic football club have been successfully consummated by the formation of the 'Glasgow Celtic and Athletic Club' under influential auspices. They have secured a six-acre ground in the east end, which they mean to put in fine order. We wish the 'Celts' all success.

In less than six months a level pitch 110 by 66 yards had been laid down, surrounded by a nineteen-feet wide track intended for cycling events, and complete with an open-air stand to accommodate nearly 1,000 persons. A rough mound around the cycling track provided rudimentary terracing. Under the stand was the pavilion, consisting of a committee room and two dressing rooms with bathroom and toilet facilities. Spectators entered by one or other of the nine gates set in the wooden barricade that ran around the ground. Admission was sixpence, women were admitted free and later on also soldiers in uniform. The official opening was set for the evening of 8 May 1888. This was also the date for the opening of the Glasgow Exhibition. The teams who played that opening game were Hibernian and Glasgow Cowlairs in front of a paying crowd of three thousand patrons. The game finished in a goal-less draw.

On Monday, 28 May 1888, Celtic in white shirts with green collars and a Celtic cross in red and green on the right breast played its first game on their own ground before two thousand spectators. The opponents in this friendly were Rangers. Celtic won 5–2. That pioneering team was: M. Dolan (Drumpellier), E. Pearson (Carfin Shamrock), J. McLaughlin (Govan Whitefield), W. Maley (Cathcart), J. Kelly (Renton), P. Murray (Cambuslang Hibs), N. McCallum (Renton), T. Maley (Cathcart), J. Madden (Dumbarton), M. Dunbar (Edinburgh Hibs) and H. Gorevin (Govan Whitefield).

The Scottish League had not yet been formed and therefore players were not tied to any particular club so were free to move at will or where their interest directed them. After this first match, Celtic joined the Glasgow and Scottish Football Associations prior to the Scottish League coming into existence in season 1890–91.

In the club's first year of existence it gave over £400 to charity and played benefit games for deserving causes in other parts of the country, the income from which was estimated at £150. The principal benefactors from this charity in the first year were £164 to the St Vincent de Paul conferences, £50 to the Whitevale Refuge and £50 to the Little Sisters of the Poor. The club donated a weekly contribution of £5 to the

Poor Children's Dinner Table in each of the three parishes of the east end. Over 250 children and a considerable number of elderly obtained a substantial daily meal as a direct consequence. The following year over £464 was donated in the same unselfish manner. In its first three years the total contribution to charity exceeded £1,200.[9]

In 1893 Brother Walfrid received orders from his Marist superiors to move to London. Little is known about him after this period, though it has been suggested that he had the idea of forming a London Celtic but decided that London's Irish population was too far and scattered across the city. On reaching the compulsory retirement age of sixty-five in 1908, Brother Walfrid had to sever his connections with St Anne's but his legacy remained in the shape of a Boy's Guild and a Young Men's Club. Walfrid's last assignment was not to the Irish but to the French. The expulsion of religious congregations from France in 1903 saw the Boarding College at Beauchamp in France closing and, as a result, it sought asylum on English soil. The French superiors entrusted Walfrid with the task of negotiating the purchase of a suitable property in the south of England in which they could house some 150 boarders and thirty brothers. Walfrid succeeded in acquiring an ideal property at Grove Ferry six miles north-east of Canterbury and around seventy miles from London. The French superiors requested that Walfrid be sent to Grove Ferry to assist the college in its organisation and development in new surroundings. The Scottish superiors granted the request and Walfrid was said to have been pleased to be of assistance as he felt he was repaying a debt to the French brothers as it was from them he had acquired his religious and professional training when preparing for his mission to Scotland. His fluency in the French language would prove to be a great asset in his new surroundings, as would his organisational skills and his natural ability in dealing with the young. It is also worth noting that it was whilst posted here that Walfrid would once again renew his acquaintance with his beloved Celtic.

In 1911, when Celtic returned from a tour overseas, Walfrid spoke to Tom Maley, a journalist with the *Glasgow Observer*. His final reported comments on Celtic were:

> Well, well, time has brought changes, outside ourselves none are left of the old brigade, I know none of the present lot of players, but they are under the old colours, and are quartered in the dear old quarters, and that suffices.

A short time later Brother Walfrid's health began to deteriorate and he was transferred to Mount St Michael's in Dumfries, the retirement house that was on the same grounds as St Joseph's College which the Brothers had opened in 1875. All the boys at the college would have known him by his name and most were ardent Celtic supporters. Apparently Brother Walfrid was invited to give lectures and on St Joseph's Day 1890 is said to have delivered a lecture on 'the picturesque abbeys of Scotland', many of which were illustrated by use of 'powerful oxy-hydrogen projection'. Walfrid's health is reported to have remained much the same during his time in Dumfries and he passed away on 17 April 1915. The following day he was buried in the Mount St Michael Cemetery.

As is typical of the Marist Brothers, there is no great elaborate remembrance to them. Through the buildings of the College, in a beautiful secluded spot, the Brothers are laid to rest in small rows. The unassuming aura is confirmed by the simple metal crosses over each grave with a sacred-heart-shaped plaque recording the name of each Brother, both their birth name and their vocational name. Indeed, there was even more than one Brother Walfrid.

The metal cross and heart for Brother Walfrid bears no reference to the great works summarised above and no mention of his pivotal role in the founding of Celtic. Simplicity pervades the site and this is a fitting setting for him and his colleagues from the Order.

Willie Maley paid him the following tribute on reflection of the great man's deeds.

He must have spent a considerable period near the Blarney stone in his young days, as his persuasive powers once experienced could never be forgotten, his work for Celtic had been a labour of love and he remained as keen as ever to hear how his 'boys', as he referred to the team, were doing.

Celtic has always been much more than a football club and part of that extra quality is the social dimension that links Celtic now and the Celtic that Brother Walfrid formed. Celtic will continue to change to meet the expectations of the supporters and business aspirations but with a social charter firmly in place it will always live up to the principles behind Walfrid's decision to form Celtic. Jock Stein always sought to impress upon the fans the importance of the founding principles of the club and the need for the fans to live up to these principles.[10]

BROTHER WALFRID

In the *Brother Walfrid Souvenir Programme 2005* Michael Kelly, Secretary, Association of Irish Celtic Supporters Clubs, wrote:

> The continued success of Celtic Football Club is the finest tribute that could be paid to Brother Walfrid. Who would have thought on that November night in 1887 that a football club established to provide funds for the Poor Children's Dinner Table would have gone on to establish a pre-eminent place in the hearts of so many supporters worldwide and among the world's elite sporting institutions? Walfrid not only helped put food on the table when he formed Celtic, he provided the exiled from Ireland with a place to 'call home' and a victimised people an opportunity to raise their spirits every weekend, proudly wear their colours, fly their flag and sing their songs. The importance of the special role the club has played for the Irish in Scotland down the years is, of course, all important and enables Celtic to stand out from all other clubs. Indeed, even today the Irish diaspora in Scotland still often finds itself marginalised and excluded from mainstream society. The story of Celtic begins with Brother Walfrid of Ballymote and bears testimony to an exiled people who faced poverty and adversity only to emerge triumphant.

Today, and forever, we thank the courage and vision of Andrew Kerins from Ballymote, Co. Sligo. His legacy to us will last forever. The memory of Brother Walfrid lives on today, not only in the history of Celtic, but in his native Ballymote where a community park and recently raised statue commemorate his name and his deeds.

The *Sligo Weekender* noted:

On Saturday, 5 November 2005, the Celtic fans came in their thousands to honour the memory of the Sligo-born Marist, Brother Walfrid, who founded Glasgow Celtic Football Club in the cause of charity on 6 November 1887.

The statue of Brother Walfrid, solely financed by Celtic supporters and magnificently created by sculptor Kate Robinson, was unveiled in front of Celtic Park and afterwards blessed by Archbishop Mario Conti of Glasgow. During the ceremonies, the Archbishop presented the Glasgow Celtic Club with a specially commissioned Celtic Cross with materials from the now demolished St Mary's Church Hall in the Calton district of Glasgow, where the Club was founded.

Irish supporters of Celtic can be especially proud to see this humble but visionary Irishman take his rightful place at the very front of Celtic Park. Brother Walfrid provided the Irish in Glasgow with a source of pride and a beacon of hope. He provided the exiled with a place they could call 'home' and a victimised people with an opportunity to raise their spirits every weekend, and proudly wear their colours, fly their flag and sing their songs.

It is with great pride to see this great Irishman take his rightful place at the front of Celtic Park. The story of the Celtic begins with Brother Walfrid and it would be fitting if all visitors to Celtic Park were to begin their 'pilgrimage' with a few moments at his feet to ponder his story and marvel at the fairytale of our cherished club, which bears testimony to the triumph of an exiled people over poverty and oppression to emerge triumphant.

Sligo will feature prominently at the unveiling in Glasgow

next Saturday of a statue honouring the founder of Celtic football club.

The statue is of the Ballymote-born Marist brother, Brother Walfrid, who is acknowledged as the driving force behind the establishment of what was to become one of the world's most famous soccer clubs.

Andrew Kerins, as he was known before entering the religious life, saw the founding of the club as a means of regular funds for his work in trying to alleviate the dreadful poverty in Glasgow at the time.

The Sligoman has of course already been similarly honoured in his native county.

In October last an eight months long fundraising campaign, promoted by the Sligo Weekender, culminated in the erection of a bronze bust of the Celtic founder in the public park in Ballymote.

That unveiling was performed by the Celtic chairman Brian Quinn and Sligo's other claim to fame at Celtic, Sean Fallon. Both will again be involved in Saturday's unveiling but they will be joined by Brother Walfrid's descendents Mary Healy and Andrew Kerins from Ballymote, who are a great grandniece and great grandnephew.

The Sligo Brother Walfrid Committee has also been formally invited by Celtic to attend the unveiling ceremony in Celtic Park at 2pm. Committee chairman Paddy Doherty, who spearheaded the Ballymote memorial campaign, said this was indeed a great honour for the Sligo committee.[11]

CELTIC FC – THE IRELAND CONNECTION

For the poor and the famished,
The Irish and their children,
For the community who came from shores of Erin
To settle in Glasgow's east end.

To raise awareness for the sick
Who had travelled on coffin ships,
Charity began from a Marist priest
As bread and water were hailed as a feast

Goodwill never shone from Scotland's heart
To those who were born under Ireland's harp,
In the church and parish, they knelt and prayed
As hope was promised from Brother Walfrid.

And when the sport of football reached the streets of Glasgow,
When poverty still grew around the man from Ballymote,
Brother Walfrid found faith for the poor and the sick
As football was introduced to, the famous Glasgow Celtic.

© **Daniel McDonagh**

3

WALFRID'S MEN OF VISION

When Edinburgh Hibernian won the Scottish Cup on 12 February 1887 by defeating Dumbarton 2–1 at Hampden Park, the seed was sown for Glasgow to have an Irish football team, just like Edinburgh. The victory was joyfully celebrated throughout Scotland by Irish communities; none more so than in the east end of Glasgow.

This, then, was the power of football and also the symbolism of success for the Irish community. Edinburgh Hibernian were feted as the victors by Glasgow's Irish and the triumphant team was taken to St Mary's Hall (where Celtic was formed some nine months later) in the Calton district of Glasgow. Amongst the rapturous throng were Brother Walfrid and John Glass. Dr John Conway led the speeches in praise of Edinburgh Hibernian and the gathering sang 'God Save Ireland'. John McFadden, the Hibernian's secretary, was so moved by the warmth of the reception and the fervour of the hospitality that he, perhaps jokingly, suggested that his hosts should 'go and do likewise!'

Brother Walfrid accepted the gauntlet of the challenge. After all, if Edinburgh could produce a successful Irish football team then surely Glasgow could do likewise, given the far greater Irish population in Glasgow.

However, Brother Walfrid would have been more than aware of the numerous Irish Catholic sides that had tried and failed in recent years to establish themselves in the Glasgow area. He would know the names well – Erin, Columba, Harp, Emerald, Hibernian and, yes, apparently even a Celtic or two. The failures of these clubs were by no means the preserve of Catholic parishes.[12]

In the poverty of Glasgow's east end Brother Walfrid would realise his real potential and his ultimate calling in life. He would take the advice of John McFadden and form a football team whose sole reason for existing would be to provide funds for the soup kitchens and 'penny dinner' tables of the east end under the assistance of the local St Vincent de Paul Societies.

His organisational powers enabled him to surround himself with the sort of people whose ideals and principles were instrumental in the founding of Celtic Football Club. Men like John Glass, James Grant, Joseph Shaughnessy, Dr John Conway, Pat Welsh, William McKillop, James Quillan, Hugh and Arthur Murphy, John O'Hara, Thomas Flood, J.M. Nellis and John H. McLaughlin.

John O'Hara and Thomas Flood led the local Catholic Union committees. J.M. Nellis and Joseph Shaughnessy were founder members of the St Aloysius Association. James Quillan and William McKillop were leading figures in the Home Government Branch in Glasgow, linked to the Home Rule Party in Ireland as were Hugh and Arthur Murphy.

John McLaughlin was a wine and spirit merchant and was

elected onto the first ever Celtic Board at the first meeting of the newly formed limited liability company on 17 June 1897. He would serve on the board until his death in August 1909, during which time he was chairman.

John O'Hara was a wine and spirit merchant who was elected onto the Celtic Board at the first meeting of the newly formed public limited liability company on 17 June 1897 in the Annfield Hall, Gallowgate. He served on the board until his death in 1905.

However, one common denominator is evident throughout the foundation process – John Glass.

John Glass was Walfrid's right-hand man. The name of John Glass repeats itself throughout research into the creation of Celtic. Undoubtedly, Brother Walfrid was the architect, the instigator, the motivator and the conduit to all the facets that would come together. John Glass, however, was the master builder and the catalyst for it all to happen. His importance should be recognised. John Glass was a joiner, a man with many contacts in the building trade and a son of Donegal. He was also, we are told, a man that could 'charm the birds down from the trees' such was his charisma. This charm and persuasiveness would be a highly useful tool in Celtic's formation, as Glass is widely acknowledged to be the man who persuaded a number of famous football players of the time to join the fledgling club. A humanitarian and a meticulous organiser, Glass was also a leader of men and, specifically, a dignified and highly respected leader of the Irish Catholic community. John Glass was the politician sitting at the round table deliberating the creation of Celtic. Glass was later described by Willie Maley as the man 'to whom the Club owes its existence'.

John Glass organised several political rallies at which Michael Davitt addressed the Highland crofters on issues of land ownership. Davitt was there as a member of the Home Rule Movement with John Glass there as a member of The Home Government Branch in Scotland. Both organisations were essentially one and the same.

He was the first President of Celtic; it was his personality which persuaded many lads to join the Celts. He was a great Irishman, ever ready to stand up for their rights, and later did much politically for the cause so dear to him. Those were not the days of written agreement and John Glass's word was always as good as any bond.

John Glass was born in Glasgow in 1851, his father was from Donegal. He was an instrumental figure in Irish and Catholic circles within Glasgow. Glass was a familiar figure at Home Government Branch meetings and at national conventions. For eleven years he was president of Celtic Football Club. John Glass died in 1906, aged fifty-five. His legacy, however, will live forever in Celtic Football Club.

Patrick Welsh was a Fenian activist in Ireland, fighting against the British Army's occupational force. In 1867, Welsh had been on the run from the British authorities, but was apprehended by a thirty-seven–year-old British soldier – Sergeant Thomas Maley of the Royal North British Fusiliers – at Dublin quay, as Welsh was attempting to flee Ireland for the prospect of a new and peaceful life in Scotland. Fortunately for Welsh, whose fate might otherwise have been imprisonment or the hangman's noose, Sergeant Maley was an Irish Catholic who had wrestled with his conscience while serving in the British Army in Ireland and there were no other witnesses on the quay to witness his capture. Welsh begged Sergeant Maley to be let go and promised he would not indulge in any further Fenian activities. Sergeant Maley turned his back and walked away. A grateful Pat Welsh boarded the waiting boat bound for the east coast of Scotland.

Pat 'the tailor' Welsh would become a master tailor with premises on fashionable Buchanan Street in Glasgow, where he would prosper both as a businessman and as a family man.

Dr John Conway was a brilliant medical student and a graduate of Glasgow University School of Medicine where he achieved the Degree of Member of the Royal College of Physicians. However, Dr Conway revoked the privilege of his middle-class upbringing and the possibility of a lucrative career as a general practitioner serving the needs of the wealthy, their warts and their addictions to opium and alcohol. Instead, Dr Conway practised medicine in Glasgow's east end. He would be kept very busy.

Diseases such as scarlet fever, whooping cough and measles decimated the young. Polio, meningitis, encephalitis, pneumonia, viral and bacterial gastroenteritis killed and maimed thousands, while alcoholism, parturient complications and transmissible sexual diseases crippled and killed the adult. All, of course, had the same root causes – inadequate nutrition and starvation, poverty and unsanitary living conditions, overly crowded ghettos, lack of education, frequent mass episodes of unemployment and the gross, indecent and inhumane disparities in Victorian, imperialist Britain between the rich and increasingly prosperous and the horrifically poor and disadvantaged. Conway must have been a man of impeccable principles to turn away from a potential life amongst privilege in order to administer to the ever so needy.

The question must therefore be asked: did the name 'Celtic' originate from this popular political influence of the day, and did Brother Walfrid and John Glass see in this name a method to celebrate Irishness, symbolise Irishness, yet simultaneously join hands with Scottish Celts? After all, historically speaking, the peoples of Ireland and Scotland were one and the same – Celts!

For Brother Walfrid, the name was as much of an embodiment of Ireland as it was Scotland and represented his new team's values perfectly. Under the guidance of Walfrid and men such as John Glass, Pat Welsh, William McKillop and John Quillan, the newly established club would move at a rapid pace and in a matter of six months succeed in leasing a patch of ground and turning it into an impressive football ground of the highest standards and facilities and capable of housing some one thousand supporters.

The organisational prowess of Brother Walfrid enabled him to bring together a group of people on 6 November 1887 in St Mary's Hall in Calton. A group of people who, like him, had suffered the displacement caused by famine and political unrest in Ireland; a group of people who had witnessed the suffering at home in Ireland and witnessed the same again in the hostile indigenous environment of Glasgow. They all had the conviction to succeed, to stand up for their Irishness. With John Glass presiding as chairman, Celtic Football Club was formed.

Before becoming a limited liability company in 1897, Celtic was formed and managed by a Committee between 1887 and

1897. The first Committee comprised of: Dr John Conway: Honorary President; John Glass: President; John O'Hara: Secretary; Hugh Darnoch: Treasurer; William Maley: Match Secretary; J. M. Nellis; Tom Maley; M. Cairns; Joseph Shaughnessy; Pat Welsh; Daniel Molloy; David Meikleham; John McDonald; William McKillop; John H. McLaughlin; Joseph McGrory and Michael Davitt: Honorary Patron.

County Mayo-born Michael Davitt was an Irish nationalist, social campaigner and founder of the Irish National League. It says much about the founding fathers of Celtic that when the club moved to its present home in 1892 Michael Davitt was asked to lay the first sod of turf. A man of great integrity and much admired for his committed stance against poverty and the bully-boy landlords of Ireland – and Highland Scotland – Davitt was a figure much revered by the Irish in Glasgow. The club further endorsed Michael Davitt and his fight for social justice when it made him an honourable Patron.

This following circular was issued in January 1888, asking for financial assistance, which came along, but not in the amount that was desired.

Circular
CELTIC FOOTBALL AND ATHLETIC CLUB
CELTIC PARK, PARKHEAD
(Corner of Dalmarnock and Janefield Streets)

Patrons
His Grace the Archbishop of Glasgow and the Clergy of St Mary's, Sacred Heart and St Michael's Missions, and the principal Catholic laymen of the East End.

CELTIC FC – THE IRELAND CONNECTION

The above club was formed in November 1887 by a number of the Catholics of the East End of the City.

The main objective of the club is to supply the East End conferences of the St Vincent De Paul Society with funds for the maintenance of the 'Dinner Tables' of our needy children in the Missions of St Mary's, Sacred Heart, and St Michael's. Many cases of sheer poverty are left unaided through lack of means. It is therefore with this principal object that we have set afloat the 'Celtic', and we invite you as one of our ever-ready friends to assist in putting our new Park in proper working order for the coming football season.

We have already several of the leading Catholic football players of the West of Scotland on our membership list. They have most thoughtfully offered to assist in the good work.

We are fully aware that the 'elite' of football players belong to this city and suburbs, and we know that from there we can select a team which will be able to do credit to the Catholics of the West of Scotland as the Hibernians have been doing in the East.

Again, there is also the desire to have a large recreation ground where our Catholic young men will be able to enjoy the various sports which will build them up physically, and we feel sure we will have many supporters with us in this laudable object.

Below is a list of those who subscribed as a result of the circular.

The following subscriptions have already been received, viz.:

His Grace the Archbishop	20s
Very Revd. Canon Carmichael	20s
Revd. F. J. Hughes	20s
Revd. A. Beyaert	20s
Revd. A. Vanderhyde	20s
Dr. John Conway	20s
Mr. John Higney	20s
Mr. James Doyle	20s
Mr. Arthur McHugh	20s
Mr. Thos. McCormick	20s
Mr. Henry Aylmer	20s
Mr. Michael Aylmer	20s
Mr. George Hughes	20s
Mr. Daniel Hughes	20s
Mr. James Quillan	20s
Mr. James McQuillan	20s
Mr. James McConnell	20s
Mr. John McGallegley	20s
Mr. John Clancy	20s
Mr. Francis Henry	20s
Mr. John Conway	20s
Mr. James Conway	20s
Mr. E. Williamson	20s
Mr. Andrew Bryan	20s

Without the wisdom, courage and vision of these great men Celtic might have been just another small team which faded into obscurity. Thanks to these 'Sons of Ireland' Celtic today is not only a football club, but an identity throughout the world with an everlasting link to Ireland.

4

EMIGRATION FROM IRELAND INTO SCOTLAND

Throughout the centuries Irish people have always left Ireland's shores for one reason or another. The mass exodus of the Catholic Irish throughout the nineteenth and twentieth centuries is well documented. Today the Irish diaspora is spread throughout the world. The diaspora who settled on Scotland's west coast, and in particular the east end of Glasgow, developed an Irish identity within that enclave of the city; an identity that is Celtic Football Club.

In 1755 Alexander Webster, an eminent divine and statistical inquirer (born in Edinburgh about the year 1707), estimated there were 16,490 Catholics in Scotland: just over one per cent of the population, most living in parts of the Highlands and the Western Isles. Despite most Catholics in Scotland living in the Glasgow/Lanarkshire areas by the turn of the millennium, several commentators have noted the presence of few in these areas at the end of the eighteenth century: only two in Lanarkshire and thirty-nine in Glasgow in the 1790s. Indicatively, there were also sixty anti-Catholic societies in Glasgow in the same period. By the middle of the Famine, the ethnic, social and religious composition of large areas of west-central Scotland was to change significantly as an estimated 100,000 Irish Catholic famine refugees fled to Scotland. In subsequent decades the attraction of employment meant many other Irish migrants chose to start a new life in Scotland as the pull of industrialisation began to reshape the condition of the economy, the Irish providing an important source of the labour required for Scottish progress.

The high point of Irish migration was 1847–1848, and some idea of the number of migrants can be conveyed in the fact that in the space of just over thirteen weeks during the summer of 1847, some 33,267 registered passengers landed from Ireland in Glasgow. It was an influx that only Liverpool could exceed, but even Liverpool's percentage of Irish-born residents (15.6%) in 1871 was surpassed by two other Scottish towns, namely Greenock (16.6%) and Dumbarton (17.7%); and there were also another four towns in Scotland apart from Glasgow (14.3%), in the 'top ten' urban centres in Britain with the largest proportions of Irish-born residents. To this immigrant mixture of denominations, classes, loyalties and age groups, Scottish towns such as Glasgow became havens, but with their high mortality rates and some of the worst slum housing in western Europe, they served as dangerous, filthy and unwelcoming 'havens' for the many Irishmen and women. The largest percentage of immigrants came from the province of Ulster, who found themselves disembarking after what was often a cramped and hazardous passage onto the Greenock, Gourock, Broomielaw, Leith or Dundee quaysides.

The Census gives the population of Scotland in 1881 as 3,735,573 and within that figure the Irish made up 218,745 or

5.8%.[13] This number, of course, does not include the second and even third generation Irish who in many cases had a heightened sense of nationality in the self-enclosed internal context of Irish immigrant society which clashed with the external context of British Scotland and its amalgam of Calvinist, Liberal and economic values.

This twin contextual system was a result of the strong identity of Irish Catholic immigrants, its defensivist ethos and its feelings of persecution both in the process of having to become 'exiles' and in their reception by Scottish society. At the same time, that society felt it was being 'swamped' by a people not only alien in race, religion, politics and culture, but actually antagonistic towards the hand that fed them. Such perceptions put up barriers which the political and factional activities of the Irish on one hand and the socio-political reaction of the Scots on the other merely reinforced. Moreover, by occupying the lowest socio-economic strata within the external context of Scottish society, the immigrants took to themselves the full panoply of class as well as ethnic grievances.

Throughout the post-Famine years of the mid-nineteenth century, especially during the first quarter of the twentieth, and more erratically for the rest of the century, substantial numbers of immigrant Irish entered Scotland, most eventually settling in the west-central belt, in and around Lanarkshire and the greater Glasgow area. Here, many towns and villages changed in their religious and social composition as the Irish poured in. Political life too was affected as the Irish brought their own experiences to mix with many Scots, particularly those of the working classes. In relation to the economic, social and political development of Scotland, the Irish and their offspring have to be considered, especially when considering such matters as: the Catholic Church; poverty; wealth; the British Labour Party and sport: especially soccer and Gaelic sports in Scotland.

By 1901, there were around 400,000 Catholics who were Irish born or who were second or third generation Irish in Scotland. Although some present day 'Irish' can trace a presence in Scotland for five or even six generations, those same people can also claim more recent forebears in that they also have a partner, parent or grandparent who are of a later wave of immigrants. These more recent immigrants almost inevitably marry into the existing Irish community, thus often reinforcing or strengthening previously lost or abandoned familial links to their country of origin.

Of course significant numbers of Irish have intermarried with other immigrant groupings as well as with the native Scots but, in areas like Coatbridge and the surrounding villages of Glenboig, Croy and Chapelhall to name a few, Irish communities remain very strong. The most common 'cultural' signifier of the Irish in Scotland has traditionally been their catholicity (although a significant number of 'Irish' coming to these parts were Protestants from the North of Ireland), symbolised by a large number of Catholic churches and schools in the Monkland area. Nonetheless, this community has a number of other features which have distinguished it from longer established neighbourhoods. This of course reflects not only the multiethnic and multi-cultural nature of modern Scotland, but particularly the Monklands and surrounding area.

There is a dearth of records relating to many aspects of the Irish in Scotland. Even today, there are few studies of that community's historical, sociological, political or contemporary experience. However, from oral evidence and newspapers, we have some idea of the recent past.

All Irish counties are represented among the Irish in Scotland. The preponderance of names like Gallacher, Kelly, Murphy, Brady, Brennan, Docherty and Donnelly gives us some idea of the origins of many local inhabitants. Likewise, other less popular names like Mahoney, Burke, Bolger and Walsh give some indication of many less well recorded areas of Ireland also sending emigrants to these parts. For example, Glenboig has a number of people whose origins lie in counties like Offaly, Westmeath and Wicklow. Current families living there of the name Walsh originate from Edenderry, County Offaly, who immigrated to Glenboig in the early twentieth century while the Cantwell family came from the village of Kilbeggan in the latter part of the nineteenth century. Some of those families called Murphy, Reilly, Johnson and Foley in Glenboig have their origins in the village of Baltinglass, County Wicklow. Others such as the Coroons (married as Burns and Hughes amongst others) of Mullingar, and Hughes of Tullamore, now living in Glenboig, reflect how groups of friends and relations emigrated from Ireland to such a small area of the Monklands, clearly attracted by the prospect of work in pits and other local industries. Today, many individuals, families and local communities in the Monklands area retain a strong sense of Irishness, conscious of the heritage given to them by their parents, grandparents and great grandparents.

Politically, culturally and in a sporting sense, the Irish have made a vast contribution to the evolution of West of Scotland society. This contribution is highlighted in the period around the turn of the twentieth century and in the early years of the new century thereafter. None more so than in the founding of Celtic Football Club by Irish immigrants.

The following statistics were noted: In 1851, 207,367 Irish born were living in Scotland, making up 7.2% of the population. In 1901, 205,064 were in Scotland making up 4.6% of the population and in 1921, 159,020 Irish born were in Scotland making up 3.3% of the population.[14]

Following the work of James Handley, on the Irish in Scotland, during the 1940s (Handley 1943; Handley 1947), 1922 is generally given as the date after which an Irish community in Scotland ceased to be properly understood as an immigrant one. This is generally explained with reference to two events. First, the service of Catholic-Irish alongside Protestant Scots during World War I, instead of in separate Catholic regiments as with recruits from elsewhere in Britain (Damer 1989, 14), was likely to have a substantial effect on the attitudes of both a Catholic community, which in many instances was Scottish-born if of Irish origin, and the Scottish-Protestant community alongside which they served. This is enhanced by the disproportionately high number of recruits coming from the Irish community even before the introduction of conscription in 1916.

Second, the outbreak of the Irish Civil War following the formation of the Irish Free State in 1921, complicated support for Irish nationalism and the prevalent association with Ireland on behalf of a Scottish-based Catholic community. Now that it was a case of Irish fighting Irish, rather than the Irish fighting the British, it was no longer so clear who to support (Gallagher

1991, 29). While undoubtedly these two events were important in realigning the allegiance of Scottish-based Catholics away from Ireland towards Scotland, they might be seen as coming towards the end of a process of shifting identification which had been taking place for some time: indeed 1922 might be seen as a rather conservative estimate.

There are ample examples in the late decades of the nineteenth century of the Irish in Scotland emphasising other characteristics in the outward expression of their community: the period 1870 to 1910, might be seen to be crucial in a transformation from the Irish in Scotland to Catholic Scots. For instance, the founding of Hibernian Football Club in Edinburgh in 1872 can be seen in stark contrast to the founding of Celtic in 1888. With one advertising its Irish connection, while requiring its players to be practising Catholics until 1893; the other adopting a name which might apply equally to Scots as to Irish, while never imposing a ban on non-Catholic players. The name Celtic could clearly apply to Scots in a way that Hibernian could not.

Further evidence of this sort can be found in the emergence of a Scottish Catholic Press, dating largely from the 1890s through the 1910s. Where any emphasis is made, the titles of these newspapers tend to place it upon Catholicism rather than Irishness. So, for example, *The Glasgow Examiner*, founded in 1895, takes as its subtitle: *the Catholic and Irish organ for Scotland*, but by 1903, the subtitle was dropped and it became simply the *Glasgow Star and Examiner*. The main Catholic press, the *Glasgow Observer*, *Scottish Catholic Herald*, and its various regional editions make no mention of Irishness at all, at least as far as their titles are concerned. Changes in the name of the *Glasgow Observer* are particularly instructive in this respect. Founded in 1885, it changed its name in 1895 to *Glasgow Observer and Catholic Herald* and in 1939 to *Glasgow Observer and Scottish Catholic Herald*. This last change may have been a response to the war with Germany and uneasiness in Britain that attached itself to Irish neutrality. Nevertheless, it is possible to see here an increasing association with Scottishness but also the suggestion that, even before 1922, the Catholic community was moving away from overt signs of Irishness.

The paradox of an immigrant Irish community attempting to assert its Scottishness by emphasising its Catholicism cannot be understated. In the face of a powerful rhetoric of Protestantism in the matrix of Scottish nationalism, the importance that religion has played, and continues to play, in attitudes towards the Irish community in Scotland is marked.

The independence of the Scottish Church is routinely identified as one of the key markers of Scottishness which can be used to justify Scottish claims of nationhood. As such, the apparent threat that the Irish in Scotland represented to the continued welfare of the Scottish churches, in the face of what was, at the time, an unparalleled decline in church attendance, had important implications for the perceived integrity of the Scottish 'nation'. Indeed the significance that religion was to obtain for the politics of the period between the wars is something that is to be emphasised.

An important example of where this was to play a key role was around the question of Section 18 of the 1918 Education (Scotland) Act. This ensured for the first time that Catholic schools would be provided for through state funding and as such brought Catholic education into the mainstream organisational structures of state education in Scotland. This was undoubtedly an important event in reorientating the Irish community's identification towards Scotland prior to 1922. It was, however, an ambiguous development, which was to have other effects.

First, it secured educational segregation which remains a thorny issue in Scottish society and is still considered by many to be a root of what sectarian antagonism still exists. Second, it provided a focus for anti-Catholic activity principally among the more extreme organisations such as the Orange Order, Scottish Protestant League and Protestant Action, which were able to mobilise around the theme 'Rome on the Rates' (Gallagher 1985; Walker 1992). It was not simply these extreme parties that chose to campaign around this issue and even the moderate John MacCormick, with the inevitable approval of Andrew Dewar Gibb, advocated the abolition of Section 18's state funding for Catholic schools as SNP policy in 1937, although this was overruled by the party (Finlay 1994, 193). Moreover, the extent of sectarian contest during elections to the School Boards was largely responsible for the transferral of their responsibilities to the County Councils in 1929 (Brown 1992, 66).

Nevertheless, the 1918 Education Act was an important event in strengthening an association with Scotland among the Scottish-based Irish and it was to have important repercussions for their relationship with Ireland. For instance, the work of Iain Patterson (co-author of Sectarianism in Scotland) on support for Irish Republican organisations from 1919–1921 would seem to indicate that the level of support these organisations received has been generally overestimated by commentators. Patterson provides evidence to suggest that financial contributions to church-organised education funds, to invest in the infrastructure of the Catholic-Scottish educational establishment, heavily outweighed donations to Republican organisations (Patterson 1993, 44). This may indicate that as an event towards the conversion from Irish immigrants to Scottish Catholics, the 1918 Education Act was more significant than the Civil War in Ireland was to be, and that the impact of the latter has perhaps been overstated.

Today, the Irish still come to Scotland in their thousands, but not as potential residents, at least not like it was in the past. Today they welcome the ferry or air crossing across the northern channel of the Irish Sea. There is no famine in Ireland to force the mass exodus as before, but yet they come. They come to the east end of Glasgow, where Brother Walfrid, John Glass and other brave Irish men faced adversity in a hostile indigenous Protestant climate and succeeded. Succeeded and gave to us the Irish and our diaspora, the legacy that is, and will continue to be, Celtic.

5

WILLIE MALEY

Without the vision and love affair that Maley had with Celtic, the club would not be where it is today, let alone exist. The Irish in Glasgow at the time, having left behind a country gripped by famine and political unrest, were living in severe poverty and misery and would have had little to inspire them.

William Patrick Maley was born on 25 April 1868 in Newry Barracks, Co. Down (formerly known as Linenhall Square and now Mourne View Park) to parents Thomas, from Ennis Co. Clare, and Mary Montgomery, Canadian-born of Scottish parents. Thomas Maley was from farming stock, born to Charles O'Malley and Susan McNamara in 1830. Thomas was a sergeant in the Royal North British Fusiliers and, although Catholic, considered joining the British Army as an astute career move.

In 1867 Thomas Maley apprehended a suspected Fenian on the quay at Dublin Port about to board a boat for Scotland. Thomas knew exactly who he was as the British Army had been searching for him for weeks. His name was Patrick Welsh. Fortunately for Welsh there was no other army presence at the port on that day to hinder Thomas Maley's conscience.

Welsh was totally distraught and in floods of tears begging to be set free and let go on his way. He promised Sergeant Maley not to indulge in any further Fenian activities if he got the chance to go to Scotland. Maley considered Welsh's words, knowing full well that Welsh faced imprisonment at best, and the gallows at worst. Without a word Thomas turned his back and walked away. A grateful Pat Welsh jumped on board the waiting boat. This incident would yield significant repercussions in the years to come.

While still in Ireland the Maley family unit was complete, with four sons, Charles, Tom, William and Alec. In 1869 Thomas Maley took 'honourable discharge' from the army and, like so many Irish, the family took the boat to Scotland, the land of his wife's family. Leaving the army and a troubled Ireland meant that he could raise his family in peace but, more importantly, he could finally conquer his conscience. With the family on its way to Scotland and an acquaintance in the ex-Fenian Pat Welsh already settled in Glasgow, prospects were looking hopeful. With an army pension secured, the Maleys were a class above most of the other Irish who had come to Scotland.

The Irish had first begun to settle in Scotland in the aftermath of the 1798 rebellion but in their masses during the famine years of 1845–1851. They firstly tended to settle on the east coast in Edinburgh but, tempted by the prospect of work, a sizeable population settled in Glasgow. They were poor, badly dressed and badly fed. Employers and landlords of slum dwellings ruthlessly exploited them.

A large Irish contingent was now living in squalor and poverty in Glasgow's east end. Unlike their unfortunate countrymen, the Maleys had a little money and in 1870 they settled in the village of Cathcart on the south side of Glasgow.

Thomas Maley was not long in Glasgow when he met Pat Welsh, who had opened a drapery shop in the city centre. Pat 'the tailor' Welsh (as he became known) offered Maley Senior a job in gratitude for his charity a few years earlier. Thomas declined the offer as he had other plans in mind to supplement his army pension. He became a drill instructor with the 3rd Renfrewshire Battalion of the Argyll and Sutherland Highlanders.

Charles, the eldest son, began to study for the priesthood, assuming the old family name of O'Malley. Tom had become a teacher; William worked as an accountant while the young Alec attended school. Tom junior had played for Third Lanark, having played for Hibernians of Edinburgh, a team exclusively for Irish Catholics. Willie went to school in Cathcart but, having no real interest in study, left at thirteen. He had picked up the skills of reading, writing and arithmetic sufficiently enough to secure employment in the printworks of Miller, Higginbotham & Co and moved onto the Telephone Company of Glasgow before a firm of chartered accountants called Smith and Wilson offered him the opportunity to train as an accountant. He worked five and a half days a week, allowing him time to study for exams. Saturdays were free, giving him the opportunity to cycle, run and play football.

On a dark December night in 1887 a knock on the door of the Maley residence in Cathcart interrupted his studies. He put down his books and answered the door. Three men stood before him. They asked to speak to Tom Maley Senior or Junior. Willie invited them in. Thomas Maley immediately recognised

Pat Welsh. His first thought was that Pat was here to ask for his support in a planned rebellion in Scotland. Their reason for calling was indeed to benefit the Irish in Scotland, but not by rebellion.

Welsh introduced the others in his company as John Glass and Brother Walfrid. They wished to speak to young Tom about playing for their newly formed football team, Celtic, formed the previous month. They had not played a game yet, but the idea of this team was to provide funds for poor Irish children in Glasgow's east end. There would be no profits and the team would consist of, although not exclusively, Irishmen. They knew Tom had played with Hibernian and felt that his inclusion would be good for the team. Thomas Senior liked the theory behind the team and, more importantly, liked the fact that it would not consist exclusively of Catholics, as was the case with Hibernian.

Tom Junior was not at home but their interest would be passed on. Willie told the visitors he also had played football, including a few games with Third Lanark Reserves. While leaving Walfrid looked at a slim athletic Willie and said 'Why don't you come along with him?'

Tom took up the invitation and Willie duly accompanied him. As a young man, Willie was much more involved in athletics than in football, although he had played a few games for Cathcart Hazelbank Juniors in 1886 and later with Third Lanark. The new club immediately caught Willie in its grasp. He trained hard with his brother and the rest of the team. Celtic Park was opened in May 1888 with a game between Edinburgh Hibernian and Glasgow Cowlairs. On 28 May Celtic played their first game, against Rangers. Both the Maleys played, with Tom scoring a hat-trick. Celtic had won their first game 5–2. The Celtic committee had learned of Willie's numerical skills and approached him about becoming secretary or treasurer. He agreed to become match secretary and soon became club secretary but wished to continue playing football.

Willie knew the club had been formed for charitable reasons and, as he looked about Glasgow's east end, the reasons were all too apparent. The children that ran about barefooted during the summer months were still barefooted when winter came. This annoyed Willie immensely.

Celtic, with both Maleys playing, found themselves in the final of the Scottish Cup in 1889 against the army team of Third Lanark. The game was a complete farce. It was played on 2 February with Glasgow covered in a blizzard and the playing surface like an ice rink. The game was declared 'a friendly', which the spectators weren't aware of until full time. It was rescheduled for the following week with Third Lanark winning 2–1. Celtic had the consolation of winning the Glasgow North Eastern Cup. Willie felt he had played well in Celtic's first competitive season but it was as match secretary where he showed his true worth. On 16 February 1889 he arranged for Celtic to travel to London to play Corinthians. A month later they went to Newcastle to play Newcastle West End, a team that would later become Newcastle United. Finally they would cross the Irish Sea to play in Belfast against Distillery and Belfast United. The Irish trip attracted huge crowds. Maley played in both games, but it was his organisational skills that ensured everything ran smoothly. He realised that the success of this tour would ensure a following for Celtic, not only in Glasgow but further afield too.

Willie, through his father, had inherited a desire for the integration of Celtic into Scottish society. Men who were all deemed to be Catholic and Irish played in Celtic's first game. Maley wanted to employ both Catholics and Protestants for Celtic's cause and, in time, integrate Celtic as a team of both a Scottish and Irish dimension. His fear was that Celtic would struggle like Hibernian, whose players were all Catholic, thus allowing those of other religions to play elsewhere. Some Hibernian players were so impressed by Maley's philosophy that they decided to join the ranks of Celtic.

Maley's feelings were that the idea to form this club was so good that it must not be allowed to become stagnant and fade out of existence. He won his first major medal when Celtic won the Glasgow Cup on 14 February 1891 beating Third Lanark 4–1.

Trouble came for Celtic in 1892 with the Irish scourge of 'landlords'. The owner of the original Celtic Park, seeing the phenomenal success of Celtic and the fact that the ground could now host internationals, decided to increase the rent from £50 to £500 per annum.

The Celtic committee decided that this was not feasible and decided instead to buy a new ground. Against all suggestions, they decided to stay rooted in the east end, where most of their supporters lived. A piece of waste ground, which consisted of a quarry hole and some derelict buildings, lay some 200 yards from their existing ground on the other side of Janefield Cemetery. It was owned by Lord Newlands, The Right Honourable James Hozier, born in 1851.

CELTIC FC – THE IRELAND CONNECTION

Celtic decided to opt for a ten-year lease with a view to eventual purchase. Maley, being an accountant, became one of the driving forces behind this. Although the site was deemed suitable, there was a huge amount of work to be done. Willie did all the costing and other necessary work to get the project going. Volunteer Irish labour filled in the quarry hole and on 19 March 1892, although not yet ready for football, Michael Davitt planted a bunch of shamrock taken from Donegal on the centre spot. The invitation of Michael Davitt was a clear indication of the Irish connections with the club.

In 1892 Celtic had become a team to be reckoned with. They won the Glasgow Cup, the Glasgow Charity Cup and the Scottish Cup. The east end of Glasgow erupted in celebration after the Scottish Cup victory. Maley was delighted that, for once, the impoverished east end had something to cheer about. As the Celtic players made their jubilant way through the east end, they realised what Celtic Football Club was all about. This was a football team like no other. This was a football club which had faced adversity and, through the vision of Willie Maley, had now succeeded. The poor of Glasgow's east end, for now at least, were laughing and cheering.

Celtic went on to win their first league championship in 1893 by one point, beating Leith Athletic 3–1 on 9 May.

Maley had achieved his ambition to play for Scotland, with his heritage on his mother's side having been deemed sufficient to allow him to turn out for Scotland. There was criticism that here was an Irishman playing for an 'Irish team' (Celtic), yet being chosen to play for Scotland against Ireland. Maley, in his administrative capacity, arranged for the game to be played at Celtic Park. Journalists were suspicious that four Celtic players (Kelly, Maley, McMahon and Campbell) were all chosen to play for Scotland. In the event, Scotland beat Ireland 6–1. Maley was retained for the game against England on 1 April at Richmond. Royalty were present in the form of the Duke and Duchess of Teck and their daughter Mary, who would later marry the future King of England, George V, and become Queen in 1910. James Kelly was captain of Scotland and he alone was introduced to the royal guests. This seemed to disturb Maley and, as revealed in later writings and conversation, he seems to have developed a dislike for royalty. Scotland was beaten by England 5–2 and Maley never played any further full internationals for Scotland, although he would feature in a Scottish League selection against the Irish League in 1894.

Professionalism had been in place in England since 1885 and, on 2 May 1893, the campaigning of Maley and the Celtic committee bore fruit to the same end in Scotland. Maley had played most of the season, although he was often hindered by injury. It was evident from supporters' views that, when he did play, he played well. He was an important factor in Celtic winning the league again in 1894. The Celtic team sheet would often include the name 'Montgomery' (his mother's maiden name), a player who looked like and played like Willie Maley. It may have been the case that his employers disapproved of one of their employees getting a second wage under the new professional ruling and hence the 'alias'.

The exploits of Willie Maley on the football pitch didn't go unnoticed. In January 1894 Sheffield United offered him the opportunity to join them. This included a job guarantee as an accountant in the Duke of Norfolk's estate. Willie pondered the offer but decided he loved Glasgow and Celtic too much to leave.

The summer of 1894 was a difficult time for Maley. On 15 May the existing committee was re-elected but Willie was accused of vote rigging. A special meeting was called for mid-June and the initial election was declared void. A re-election was called for by a show of hands. One hour after they were deposed, Maley and his committee were re-elected. This incident showed Maley in a bad light, although he had always claimed his innocence and honesty in all his dealings. No effort was ever made to depose Maley from his position as secretary, but it did show that all was not harmonious at Celtic Park. Season 1894/95 was difficult for him, particularly when things didn't go well on the field. Maley himself was struggling with injury and loss of form. He wanted to retire from playing and concentrate on his administrative role and his other business interests. He played in Celtic's record victory on 26 October 1895 when Celtic beat Dundee 11–0.

On 6 February 1896 he married his long-term sweetheart, Helen Pye, in the Gorbals. Together they had two sons but, sadly, it was not the happiest of marriages. She was to take second place to football and his unquestionable love for Celtic. They lived at 38 Whitevale Street, Glasgow. On 24 February 1896, he joined Manchester City on a month's loan. Wages were somewhat better in England. A month later he returned to Glasgow having played just one game for City. On 7 May 1896, Willie's father Thomas sadly died of pneumonia at the age of sixty-six. This was a bitter blow for Willie. He was devoted to his father and everything he had achieved was through his father's teaching and beliefs. At the end of the

1896 season, Willie made it clear to his fellow committee members that his playing days were over. He was happy, however, to continue in his role as secretary. With his football days over, Willie devoted his spare time to his other love, athletics. He had run for the Clydesdale Harriers years earlier but had turned his back on them for football. On 26 June 1896 at Hampden Park, Willie became the 100–yard champion of Scotland. He also did a great deal of cycling but as an amateur. Willie did, however, bring many cyclists to the track at Celtic Park for competition. He also served on the committee of the Scottish Amateur Athletic Association for thirty years, eventually becoming president.

Maley, like others, realised that if Celtic was to continue in the line of its founding fathers and provide food and clothing for the poor of the east end, then it must now operate as a business. In this way, all profits could be directed into the east end cause. The internal dealings involved to set up Celtic as a business are unclear but, in 1897, the board of Celtic directors asked Willie Maley at the age of twenty-nine to become secretary / manager on a salary of £150 per annum. Maley was given the opportunity to run the club as he saw fit, overseeing signings and administration. He was, however, always answerable to his board, which seldom failed to support him. For the next forty years Mr Willie Maley would be Mr Celtic. Although not yet thirty years of age, Maley was where he wanted to be, running the club he loved. He had money at his disposal, as Celtic's methods of generating capital were phenomenal.

Internationals were now held at Celtic Park as well as athletics and cycling, within which Willie would sometimes participate. Maley was well aware what Celtic had achieved in less than ten years of existence. He was determined about two things to ensure the survival and success of Celtic: players must be adequately paid and must train and play hard but, more importantly, they had to think football, they had to think Celtic. They had to be committed to the club and to its supporters, who were, after all, the reason why the club was formed. They had to realise how fortunate they were to play for, in Maley's words the 'greatest team on Earth'.

His much used quote to players was:

> It's an honour and a privilege to wear those green and white jerseys. Those people out there have given a lot to see you wearing those stripes [Celtic wore green and white vertical stripes until 1903]. What are you going to give them back?

His philosophy (possibly coming from his father) was that players didn't have to be a Roman Catholic to play for Celtic. He often said 'It is not his creed or his nationality which counts – it's the man himself'.

On 28 November 1898 William Patrick Maley Junior was born. Maley now had two sons and nurtured the hope that they too would one day play for Celtic and Scotland. His hopes were very much in vain as neither possessed the slightest ability for football. Domestic problems caused Willie to leave his wife and sons in Whitevale Street and move to a house in Partick. There is no evidence to support the idea that he was a womaniser; he and his wife simply decided that they would be better off apart. In the census of 1901 Helen Maley is described as being head of the house in Whitevale Street with Willie Maley being elsewhere.

Scotland's large Irish population was already bought over by the enormity of Celtic and provided a large amount of talent to the team. Maley was given approval to scout the British Isles for talent, as money was available. He could sign players of any religion. With his football brain, he couldn't fail. In season 1897/98, Celtic won the league by a distance, going through the entire campaign undefeated. In the interim, times were bleak with Rangers winning four league titles in a row. In 1901 Maley considered the fact that, instead of buying players elsewhere, he should concentrate on bringing on youngsters already on the books.

The team had come far in thirteen years, but Maley realised it could not stand still. It must develop and go for more success. Maley had a spy network active under his instruction to create the greatest team Scotland had ever seen. Rangers had won the league four times in succession and although the Scottish Cup at the time brought more prestige, it was the league that determined which was the most consistent team on the pitch.

He stated himself:

> But our directors were by no means idle. They included men who knew football, and would not be satisfied until they had built up a side which was capable of producing and main-taining the standard of their great predecessors.

This showed the modesty of Willie Maley as it was he who had built up the side and the directors never failed to back him. In the early 1900s, with his spy network gathering pace, he signed some of the greatest players to wear the Celtic jersey: James (Napoleon) Quinn; Willie Loney; David Hamilton; James McMenemy; Alec Bennet; James (Sunny Jim) Young; Bobby Muir; James Hay; Alec McNair and Peter Sommers.

Rome was not built in a day and neither was Maley's Celtic team, but this great team virtually won everything between 1904 to 1910. The Scottish Cup final of 1902 was lost to Hibernian with the final played at Celtic Park. Ibrox was to host this final with Hampden getting a makeover but, with the first Ibrox disaster having occurred a few weeks earlier, when twenty-six people were killed after a wooden stand collapsed during a Scotland v England international, it had to be played at Celtic Park. At the end of season 1902, Celtic, Rangers, Sunderland and Everton took part in the Glasgow Exhibition / Ibrox Disaster Trophy for the victims of this disaster. Rangers put the Exhibition Trophy forward for this tournament with them having won it in a one-off competition in 1901. The assumption was that the winners would hand back the trophy to Rangers. Celtic beat Rangers 3–2 in the final but Maley refused to hand back the trophy. Celtic had won the competition and they fully intended to keep the trophy.

The fruits of Willie Maley's hard work began to pay dividends on 16 April 1904. It was the final of the Scottish Cup at the newly enlarged Hampden Park – the first Scottish Cup final that would see Celtic wearing the now familiar 'hoops'. Celtic defeated Rangers 3–2 with Jimmy Quinn scoring a hat-trick. After season 1913/14, Maley took Celtic on its customary summer tour of Europe. He was always keen that Celtic would be the ambassador for Scotland, the Irish diaspora and the game. The Germans had always been hospitable to Celtic on previous tours, perhaps, as Maley noted, because they saw Celtic as representing Ireland and Scotland and could understand how both 'celtic' nations had suffered. Maley was on holiday in the Highland village of Tomintoul when he read of the assassination of Archduke Ferdinand on 28 June 1914. Worrying for Maley was the fact that some of his own Glasgow Irish community were beginning to talk of war. He thought that when the football season would resume on 1 August the talk of war would be gone. Sadly, war arrived before the football.

Maley now found himself in a difficult position. On one hand he felt he had to be patriotic, given his father's military background and his absolute determination that the Irish in Scotland play their role in maintaining the British Empire. On the other hand, he had no desire to harbour any war-like feelings towards the Germans, with whom he had met and played against so recently. Almost immediately, player's wages were cut to £2. Maley, through his influence and contacts, ensured his best players got work in and around Glasgow to supplement the 'wage restriction'. He was not keen on his players becoming part of the war machine. Soldiers would use Celtic Park on match days for recruitment purposes. The idea of clean barracks, good wages and regular food was appealing to the undernourished and underprivileged.

On Friday, 9 November 1917, Willie received a telegram stating that Father Charles O'Malley had suffered a heart attack in Ayr and had died. Father O'Malley was Willie's eldest brother by eight years, having being born in 1859. Charles had trained for the priesthood in Nottingham but, having no great love for football, he would only occasionally go to Glasgow to see Celtic play.

The 1920s were a difficult period for Willie Maley, a time when he would sometimes lose his grip on things. The war was over but he found that there existed a clash between his Victorian ideals and the new developments that were taking place. What he had achieved for Celtic was permanent. Now in his fifties and part of the older generation, he failed to recognise the changes that were taking place. The war was won but at a severe cost to resources and wealth. The working man was no longer willing to accept things as they were. They had fought and won and were not going be to be dictated to by employers any more. With the Labour Party in government in 1924, and with industrial unrest in Glasgow (and indeed throughout Britain), the working man had found a voice.

If Willie felt he could return to his mantle of 'Mr Celtic', as he was in the early 1900s, then he was gravely mistaken. There was a new generation of professional footballer who would fail to comply with the Victorian ideals of Willie Maley. Many failed to answer his line of thought and left.

Maley has always portrayed the Celtic support as being devoid of hooliganism, but Monday, 26 April 1920 was a dark day. Dundee had succumbed to Rangers 6–1 two days previously, which effectively handed Rangers the league. The Celtic support claimed Dundee had not tried hard enough. Dundee was verbally harassed from the start and, with the game at 1–1, the crowd invaded the pitch. Some of the Dundee players and referee were assaulted. Alec McNair and Joe Cassidy of Celtic seemed to appease the violence but Maley was embarrassed and disturbed by the whole incident. He was, however, on the committee of the Scottish League at the time (being president from 1921–1924) and had some success in hushing up the nasty affair. Rangers won the league and Dundee decided against pursuing the matter. Celtic was instructed to play its first three games of the following season away from home as a token punishment.

In 1922 the Celtic board took the disastrous decision to axe the reserve team; a decision made by a board which had always followed Willie's decisions. Possibly a younger and more stubborn Maley would have dug his heels in. The decision may have been down to wages. Money was never far from the mind of Willie Maley. He believed that the professional footballer had a much better life than the average working man and indeed earned more. His underlying belief was always that it was an honour to play for Celtic. The result of this 'money pinching' was a switch in supremacy to the south-west of the city (Rangers), a supremacy that would exist until the end of his career. In 1931 the decision was reversed and a reserve team was entered into the Alliance League. Parkhead, with its new stand, looked considerably better than it had done for years. Attendances were as best as could be expected for a time of recession. On 11 April 1931, 104,000 packed into Hampden Park as Celtic beat Motherwell 4–2 in the final of the Scottish Cup.

Willie Maley would often reflect on that night in December 1887 when, along with his brother Tom, he was invited by Brother Walfrid, John Glass and Pat Welsh to join in the forma-tion of Celtic Football Club, a club formed to assist the Irish in Glasgow through its charitable work. Celtic was Maley's life: 'This club has been my life and I feel without it my existence would be empty indeed.'

In the latter years of the 1930s he thought about retiring. But what would he do to spend his days? At the club's Jubilee Dinner at the Grosvenor Hotel, Glasgow, on 16 June 1938, Willie arrived slightly late so those in attendance could clearly see him as he made his way to the top table. He sat attentively as club representatives heaped praise upon him. Celtic chairman, Tom White, presented him with a cheque of 2,500 guineas, fifty for each year of service. A small reward, perhaps, for what he had achieved for Celtic. This 'golden handshake' would see him comfortable for the rest of his life and it was widely felt that the time was right for Willie Maley to leave Celtic.

Willie heaped his own praise on those who had assisted him in bringing Celtic to these huge heights. He was last to leave the hotel. The evening had been a celebration of the first glorious fifty years of Celtic. A fitting celebration, as Celtic and Willie Maley were indistinguishable. In retrospect, it might have been better if he had stood down on that night and allowed someone fresh to take over since, during his last eighteen months at Parkhead, Maley for the first time in his life seemed to be suffering from a prolonged illness. It was felt that his obsession with money had become unhealthy and he was often unwilling to spend club funds. It was a constant gripe of players that their counterparts at Ibrox were much better paid. Celtic had come a long way since that first meeting on 6 November 1887 when an institution was formed to provide food for the Irish children of the east end. It had become a successful football team under the direction of Willie Maley.

In season 1938/39 Maley found himself isolated by both players and board. Players were looking for bonuses for competing in certain competitions, which he refused to pay. On the board side, he was asked to pay income tax on the gift of 2,500 guineas, which he fully expected his directors to pay. Everyone suffered. Maley took ill, an undefined illness then, but which was thought to be depression. The form of the team plummeted. At Parkhead on 30 December 1938, the directors decided enough was enough. The game was against Motherwell and ended 2–2. It caused supporters much distress and, not for the first time that season, a slow handclap could be heard. On New Year's Day 1940 it was made public that Willie Maley would depart Celtic on 1 February At the end of season 1939/40 he would write:

> Personally I can never forget the 1939/40 season. It has been to me the end of my football career and has robbed me of the very tang of life. Football has been my thoughts morning, noon and night for all the fifty-two years I have been in it, and it has been hard to drop out of my regular ways.

Celtic supporters took the news but they had other things to occupy their thoughts: World War II. By the middle of February 1940, Jimmy McStay was in charge. It would be over a decade before Willie Maley would set foot in Parkhead again. His life was very low profile after Celtic. Such had been the intensity of the feud with the Celtic board that he was not seen at Parkhead again until 10 August 1953. That day Celtic played a Bohemians Select team for the 'Willie Maley Testimonial Fund' in aid of the Grampian sanatorium in Kingussie, in the Scottish Highlands. He was welcomed with applause back to the ground he loved so much by the Celtic fans who had never forgotten his great success. He was now eighty-five years of age but walked to the centre of the pitch with some of his former players, including Joe Dodds, Jimmy McMenemy and Willie Loney. Maley had made the peace and would be at Parkhead as often as his health would permit to watch his beloved Celtic.

On Wednesday 2 April 1958, Willie Maley died in a nursing home at 32 Mansion House Road in Glasgow. He was eighty-nine.

Cyril Horne in the *Glasgow Herald* wrote the following day:

Celtic FC was his life. Many of the players who served under him had mixed feelings about the discipline Mr Maley exerted, but I do not know one who at the end of his career did not concede that he had been correct. He was not merely, however, a man of stern discipline and distinctive judgement in football matters. There was no greater sentimentalist, no kinder man. The good deeds that he did were known only to a few outwith the recipients and then almost always because they in their appreciation referred to them in later years. It is unlikely that Celtic Football Club will ever have a greater Celt.

His funeral was held on Good Friday, 4 April in St Peter's Church, Hyndland and he was later buried in Cathcart Cemetery.

The following day, a minute's silence was observed and black armbands worn, both at Pittodrie, where Celtic beat Aberdeen 1–0, and at Parkhead, where Clyde beat Motherwell 3–2 in the Scottish Cup semi-finals. For days to come, the press was full with tributes to the great man. Everyone seemed to agree on one thing though, that Celtic would never have amounted to anything without him at the helm.[15]

Willie Maley was, and still is, the longest serving manager at Celtic. In his forty-three years as manager he won nineteen league titles, fifteen Scottish Cups, fourteen Glasgow Cups and nineteen Glasgow Charity Cups.

The man from Newry, Co. Down, Ireland had done it all, for Celtic. It is a fitting tribute and appreciation of a man who has been dead for fifty years that he is still so fondly remembered by Celtic fans.

Willie Maley was his name
He brought some great names to the game
When he was boss at Celtic Park,
Taught them how to play football
Made them greatest of them all
Gallacher and Quinn have made their mark.

Oh, they gave us Jimmy McGrory and Paul McStay
Johnstone, Tully, Murdoch, Auld and Hay,
And most of the football's greats have passed through
    Parkhead's gates
To play football the Glasgow Celtic way.

6

THE IRISH TRICOLOUR
AND FLAG ISSUE OF 1952

Because of the direct association with Ireland through its founders, Celtic Football Club, from its very formation, has always flown the Irish flag over its place of play. In 1888 it was the original Irish flag, a golden harp on a green background. The unofficial Irish flag, served from 1798 until the early twentieth century as a symbol of nationalism. As the revolutionary James Connolly wrote, just weeks before he participated in the quixotic Easter Rebellion of 1916 that led to his execution by firing squad in Kilmainham Jail, Dublin on 12 May 1916:

> For centuries the green flag of Ireland was a thing accurst and hated by the English garrison in Ireland, as it is still in their inmost hearts . . .
>
> . . . the green flag of Ireland will be solemnly hoisted over Liberty Hall as a symbol of our faith in freedom, and as a token to all the world that the working class of Dublin stands for the cause of Ireland, and the cause of Ireland is the cause of a separate and distinct nationality.
>
> —*Worker's Republic,* 8 April, 1916

THE IRISH TRICOLOUR AND FLAG ISSUE OF 1952

The oldest known reference to the use of the three colours (green, white and orange) as a nationalist emblem dates from September 1830 when tricolour cockades were worn at a meeting held to celebrate the French revolution of that year – a revolution which restored the use of the French Tricolour. The colours were also used in the same period for rosettes and badges and on the banners of trade guilds. There is also one reference to the use of a flag striped with orange and green alternately. However, the earliest attested use of an Irish Tricolour flag was in 1848 when it was adopted by the Young Ireland movement under the influence of another French revolution. An historian named Dermot Power has established that the Tricolour was publicly unveiled by Thomas Francis Meagher, a leader of the Young Ireland movement, at a meeting in his native city of Waterford on 7 March 1848. The report showed the large second-floor window in The Wolfe Tone Club from which he addressed a crowd in the street below and at which the flag was displayed. The National Flag of Ireland (*An Bhratach Náisiúnta*), also known as the Irish Tricolour, is the national flag of the Republic of Ireland. The flag was first adopted as the national flag of the Irish Free State in 1922. When the Free State was succeeded by the state now known as the Republic of Ireland, under the 1937 Constitution of Ireland the Tricolour was given constitutional status.

The Tricolour is regarded by many as the national flag of the whole of Ireland. Thus it is flown (often controversially) by many nationalists in Northern Ireland as well as by the Gaelic Athletic Association (GAA). Historically Ireland has been represented by a number of other flags, including St Patrick's Cross, and the 'four provinces' flag.

From 1783 to 1922, the usual flag used to symbolise Ireland officially was known as 'Saint Patrick's Cross'. This consisted of a red saltire on a white field. It was the symbol of the Order of St Patrick, and was incorporated into the Union flag following the 1801 union of Great Britain and Ireland. The flag however was never accepted or liked by a majority of the Irish people, who saw it as a British invention. The pattern on St Patrick's flag clearly resembles Saint Andrew's cross in the flag of Scotland. It may have been adopted from the arms of the Earls of Kildare (the Fitzgerald family). An Irish coin from the 1480s has two saltires on it. A map of the 1601 battle of Kinsale shows a combined Irish/Spanish force under a red saltire. The seal of Trinity College, Dublin, from the same period, shows the saltire under a harp, opposite Saint George's cross under a lion. Two Dutch seventeenth-century guides also described it as the Irish flag.

Today the plain St Patrick's cross is rarely seen, although of course it remains ubiquitous as one of the components of the Union flag of the UK. It is occasionally used as a neutral flag, for the representation of Ireland, in Northern Ireland. It is the basis of the police badge of the new Police Service of Northern Ireland and is also used by the Reform Movement in the Republic.

The tricolour was first used by Irish nationalists in 1848 during the Young Irelanders' rebellion, though the colours on the original flag were in reverse order to the modern version. Inspired by the French Tricolour and the Newfoundland Tricolour, it was designed to represent the Catholic majority (represented by green) and the Protestant minority (represented by orange due to William of Orange) living together in peace (symbolised by the white band). Contrary to popular myth, the Tricolour was not the actual flag of the Easter Rising, although it had been flown from the GPO; that flag was in fact a green flag with a harp and had the words 'Irish Republic'. However the Tricolour became the *de facto* flag of the extra-legal Irish Republic declared in 1919 and was later adopted by the Irish Free State.

The 1922 Free State Constitution did not provide for national symbols. The modern Constitution of Ireland provides in Article 7 that the 'national flag is the tricolour of green, white and orange'. Today the European flag is flown alongside the national flag on all official buildings, and in most places where the Irish flag is flown over buildings. The National flag is flown over *Áras an Uachtaráin* (the residence of the President of Ireland); Leinster House (the seat of the Irish parliament), when parliament is in session; and Irish courts and state buildings. The Tricolour is also draped across the coffins of presidents and ex-presidents of Ireland; soldiers and Garda (Irish police) personnel killed in the line of duty and other notable recorded state funerals, such as Roger Casement in 1965, or Kevin Barry in 2000, when he was re-interned.

USE IN NORTHERN IRELAND

The purported symbolism of the flag (peace between Catholics and Protestants) has not become a universal reality. In 1920, Ireland was partitioned, with the unionist-dominated north-east becoming Northern Ireland, while later, in 1922, the remainder of Ireland seceded from the United Kingdom of Great Britain and Ireland as the Irish Free State.

Northern Ireland continued to use the British Union flag and created its own derivation of the flag of Ulster (with a crown on top of a six-pointed star) to symbolise the state. Furthermore, for many years the Tricolour was effectively banned in Northern Ireland under the Flags and Emblems Act of 1954 which empowered the police to remove any flag that could cause a breach of the peace but specified that a Union flag could never have such an effect. In 1964, the enforcement of this law by the RUC at the behest of Ian Paisley involved the removal of a single Tricolour from the offices of Sinn Fein in Belfast and led to two days of rioting. The Tricolour was immediately replaced, highlighting the difficulty of enforcing the law.

Despite its original symbolism, in Northern Ireland the tricolour, along with most other markers of either British or Irish identity, has come to be a symbol of division. The Ulster Unionist Party Government of Northern Ireland adopted the flag of Northern Ireland (based on the flag of Ulster) in 1953. Thus it is this flag and the Union flag that are flown by unionists, while the Tricolour is often used to represent nationalist defiance.

In Northern Ireland each community uses its own flags, murals and other symbols to declare its allegiance and mark its territory, often in a manner that is deliberately provocative. Kerbstones in unionist and loyalist areas are often painted red, white and blue, while in nationalist and republican areas kerbstones may be painted green, white and orange. Elements of both communities fly their flag from chimneys and tall buildings.

Under the 1998 Belfast Agreement, flags continue to be a

source of disagreement in Northern Ireland. The Agreement states that:

All participants acknowledge the sensitivity of the use of symbols and emblems for public purposes and the need in particular in creating the new institutions to ensure that such symbols and emblems are used in a manner which promotes mutual respect rather than division.

Nationalists have pointed to this to argue that the use of the Union flag for official purposes should be restricted, or that the Tricolour should be flown alongside the British flag on government buildings. Unionists argue that the recognition of the 'principle of consent' (i.e. that Northern Ireland's constitutional status cannot change without a majority favouring it) by the signatories amounts to recognizing that the Union flag is the only legitimate official flag in Northern Ireland.

There are a few reasons why green is associated with Catholics in Ireland, emerging from the long struggle for independence. Around the time of the American Revolution, there was anxiety in the ruling classes of Europe; fearing that the ideas of liberty and so on would spread to their own population and spark some kind of revolt. This was very true in Ireland, where resentment to British rule was very strong. Green had always been associated with Ireland as a nation, and with the revolutionary groups within it. For a while around 1776, the wearing of the colour green was actually barred by the authorities, giving rise to the song of the same name, 'The Wearing of the Green'.

Green was the colour of sympathy for independence around this time and has pretty much stuck with that until this day. The modern flag arrived much later, as a compromise flag, which, ironically, is used today as a symbol for (complete) independence.

Jim McBrearty, 29 April 2003

The orange colour is associated with the Protestants in Ulster and that derived from William III (of the House of Orange) who defeated the Irish Catholics at the Battle of the Boyne in 1690. It was included in the Irish flag in an attempt to reconcile the Protestants with the Irish independence movement.

A.P. Burgers, 26 May 2004

In 1922, when Ireland became a 'Free State', the new flag of the Irish Republic, the modern Tricolour was presented to Celtic by the Free State Government on behalf of the Irish people. The tricolour as we see it today now flew over Celtic Park and was clearly visible throughout the east end of Glasgow. Rarely has a flag possessed such relevance as that of the Tricolour, the national flag of the Republic of Ireland. It may have just been a 'flag' as witnessed by any spectator or visiting team to Glasgow's east end, but the fact that this was the flag of the Republic of Ireland seemed to weigh heavily on the minds of the Scottish Football governing body.

An official of long-standing service within this governing body of Scottish football, Harry Swan, chairman of Hibernian (the first non-Catholic to hold the post at Hibernian) seems to have been the prime agitator for its removal.

Although both clubs were of Irish origin, there would appear to have been some bad blood present. This would most certainly have stemmed from the early years in the history of Celtic when professionalism was not yet introduced in Scotland and players were not tied to any particular club. John Glass, who had seen the financial contribution that Celtic had made to the charity work of Brother Walfrid, would often entice Hibernian players to play for Celtic, sometimes in controversial circumstances, as the Hibernian board had seen it.

When Scotland played Ireland at Parkhead on 16 September 1934, an official representing the Scottish Football Association approached Celtic at the request of the Irish Football Association to ask that the flag be removed. It may have been the same official at 'dirty' work again in 1952 when Celtic was threatened with expulsion from the league lest they remove 'the flag'.

The Tricolour had being flying over Celtic Park since 1922. Jimmy McGrory, Celtic manager 1945–65, asked for it to be taken down prior to a tour of Ireland in 1951 to be washed. It almost fell apart, tattered and worn after thirty years of Glasgow weather. He approached numerous flag makers in Scotland in an attempt to have it repaired, none of whom would touch an Irish flag let alone repair it. Correspondence followed to Eamon deValera (Irish President) in which Jimmy outlined the plight of the flag. De Valera promptly replied with a gift from the Irish people, a new Tricolour. A grateful McGrory accepted the gift and once again the Irish Tricolour flew proudly over 'Paradise', the term used to describe the relocation of Celtic to the existing stadium – moving from beside the Janefield Street Cemetery was like moving from hell (the scourge of the landlord) into Paradise.

CELTIC FC – THE IRELAND CONNECTION

On 1 January 1952, the Ne'erday game between Celtic and Rangers was marred by violence. Bottles were thrown, eleven spectators were arrested and others fined for incidents, which occurred in and around Celtic Park. The Glasgow magistrates made proposals and the Scottish Football Association and the Scottish Football League were asked to consider them:

1 That the Celtic and Rangers clubs should not again be paired on New Year's Day when, it was suggested, passions were likely to be inflamed by drink and when bottles were more likely to be carried than on any other day.

2 That on every occasion when those clubs meet admission should be by ticket only and the attendance limited to a number consistent with public safety, the number decided by the chief constable.

3 That in the interests of safety of the public Celtic FC should be asked to construct numbered passageways in the terracing at each end of Celtic Park.

4 That the two clubs should avoid displaying flags which might incite feelings among spectators.

In conclusion to these guidelines, the committee further instructed Celtic to refrain from displaying in its park on match days any flag or emblem which had no association with Scotland or the game.

In response to the administrator's proposals, Robert Kelly, Chairman of Celtic, stated that the Scottish Football Association had no power to make such an order. In support of the Celtic chairman, J. F. Wilson, Chairman of Rangers, concluded that the flag had never been of any annoyance to Rangers. All in attendance at administrative level admitted that the flag was not the cause of the disturbances. A motion offered by acting president of the Scottish Football Association, H. S. Swan, chairman of Hibernian, was that Celtic was offered three days to remove the flag or face suspension. It was raised that if such a motion was carried, which Celtic would duly ignore, then the league programme would suffer as well as several other clubs. The referee committee, acting on its own merit, felt that ordering Celtic to remove the flag was not inflicting a punishment on the club but was simply an attempt to stop violence at football matches. Robert Kelly was asked time and time again during discussions to realise that that was the only motive.

Kelly struck a blow for Celtic when he said that 'In the history of Scottish football suspension had only been ordered when a rule had been broken, and no one had proven that Celtic had broken any rule'.

Celtic was instructed by the committee to refrain from displaying at Parkhead any flag or emblem which had no association with Scotland. It was noted that the corner flags were emblazoned with shamrocks and the ball boys wore green, white and orange uniforms. The committee also took exception to the fact that an occasional Celtic jersey of the time consisted of a white shirt with green sleeves and a shamrock on the breast.

Other clubs were asked to guard against a continuation of the ban. One such club was Hibernian, founded in 1875 by Canon Edward Hannon, which had a large harp patterned on a red brick wall of a stand at its ground. This was removed by H. S. Swan.

Three weeks before the date fixed for judgement on the flag, the Scottish Football Association altered the issue. On 7 April 1952 the football governing body decided to cancel its order for the time being. The acting chairman of the referee committee, who had instructed Celtic to remove the Tricolour, proposed that his decree be suspended until the outcome of a meeting between the Scottish League and the Scottish Football Association for the purpose of reconsidering the matter. A few days before the opening of season 1952/53, a council meeting of the Scottish Football Association, convened by the president (H. S. Swan), was defeated by eighteen votes to twelve. Thus was cancelled what was probably the most ridiculous order ever given in football legislation.[16]

And today still, as it was from the beginning, the Irish flag flies proudly over Celtic's place of play.

7

THE IDENTITY OF CELTIC

An article written by Dr Joseph Bradley titled 'Celtic Football Club, Irish Ethnicity, and Scottish Society' printed in the *New Hibernia Review* in 2008 said that John Hoberman observes in *Sport and Ideology* (1984) that 'Sport has no intrinsic value structure, but it is a ready and flexible vehicle through which ideological associations can be reinforced', and Eric Hobsbawm asserts that 'The identity of a nation of millions seems more real as a team of eleven named people'. Implicit in these comments is the belief that sport has the capacity to embody and express identity and community – in its national, cultural, ethnic, religious, social, political, and even economic dimensions – in a way that few other social manifestations can match. Celtic Football Club in Scotland, a professional soccer team based in Glasgow, offers a vivid case study of these observations and assertions, including aspects of the nature of community and supporter associations involved in Scottish football. For countless supporters, Celtic is far more than 'merely' a football club. As an institution founded by and for the Irish Catholic immigrant diaspora in the West of Scotland, the role of Celtic Football Club in the cultural and ethnic identity of this part of the Scottish population warrants attention for a number of reasons.[17]

In its beginning, Celtic provided money to feed the poor in the immediate vicinity of the east end of Glasgow and became a symbol for Irish Catholics in the West of Scotland. The club helped give the community self-respect and encouraged it to hold its head up amidst much deprivation, degradation and hostility. The Irish responded by making Celtic part of their very being. Today, songs sung by the Celtic support like 'The Fields of Athenry' and 'Let the People Sing' are reminders of the roots and the identity of Celtic and its dedicated fans.

Celtic has never been closed-minded. We have always been an open club and never discriminated against non-Catholic players. Celtic has always been the standard bearer for Irish Catholic immigrants in Scotland, but those not of that background have always been welcome to support us.

In 1887/88 the Irish community in the east end of Glasgow celebrated its roots, heritage and identity by giving birth to Celtic Football Club. In 1967 this immigrant community in Scotland gained the respect of the football world by winning the world's premier club trophy, the European Cup. Hopefully this community, and those who wish to share in our team's glories regardless of background, have many more celebrations to come. Celtic belongs to us, and those who for ninety minutes want to share something with us.

However, there does sadly exist in Scotland a sectarian rivalry. Sectarianism has been widely condemned as a cancer in Scottish society that has divided communities and cost lives for generations. The nation's leading football clubs, Rangers and Celtic, often stand accused of being magnets for bigotry. Some authors consider that the root of sectarianism in Scotland actually comes in the form of anti-Catholicism and anti-Irishness.

There is animosity towards the flying of the Irish Tricolour that persists to this day. Dr Joseph Bradley believes trying to ban traditional symbols of Irishness only serves to fuel sectarian tensions.

> They see themselves as a community partly under siege and in continual conflict because of the dilution of their identity. The idea of trying to get these people to conform to a view of Scottishness that suits the majority is not the way forward. A degree of loyalty has to be given to the state that people live in but there are other cultural things that matter on a daily basis.
>
> You should be able to express your primary identity. When we see people flying the Tricolour or the Union Flag, we shouldn't get it out of proportion. Rangers and its supporters also have every right to assert their British identity.[18]

Willy Maley, professor of English literature at Glasgow University, agreed that past anti-Catholic and anti-Irish attitudes in Scotland had fuelled sectarianism. 'If you back people into a corner and take away their symbols of identity it polarises opinion and makes sectarian violence more probable,' he said. 'If you try to ban something then everyone wants it. It breeds monsters. Recognising those symbols as legitimate should reduce tensions.'

One man who has been at the sharp end of the sectarian debate in Scotland is Donald Findlay, the Glasgow QC who stepped down as Rangers' vice-chairman in 2000 after being caught on film singing 'The Sash', a song that commemorates a famous Protestant victory over Catholic forces in Ireland. Findlay said in the past he had defended the right of Celtic fans to fly the Tricolour as much as Rangers' fans right to display the Union flag.

> There remains sectarian hatred in the hearts and minds of a minority, but I believe they are becoming less likely to shout with pride of their bigotry. And those of us who speak out, those who reject the notion that one tradition, a belief in one faith, leads to a loathing of another are beginning to make a difference. And with our rejection of hatred within a faith we can also speak up for understanding and common cause between faiths. Scotland is a country of many faiths – and of none. And there is room here for a healthy mix of people, cultures and religions.
>
> *Jack McConnell*, 18 May 2004

The competition between Celtic and Rangers has roots in more than just a simple sporting rivalry. It is infused with a series of complex disputes, sometimes centred on religion (Catholic and Protestant) and Northern Ireland-related politics (Loyalist and Republican). The result has been an enduring enmity between fans that has extended beyond the kind of intra-city football rivalry that might be expected in situations where two clubs dominate a country's football scene. This has been manifested in a history laden with sectarian violence, sometimes leading to deaths.

In 1996, Jason Campbell, a twenty-year-old Protestant,

was convicted of the unprovoked murder of sixteen-year-old Mark Scott, who was wearing a Celtic jersey, although covered by a jacket at the time. Campbell waited until Scott had walked past the bar doorway in which he was standing, sneaked up behind Scott and cut his throat with a carpet fitter's knife. Scott died instantly. Subsequent floral tributes to the youth laid at the spot of his murder were defaced and destroyed by Loyalists and Rangers fans. After being convicted, Campbell applied to be transferred to The Maze Prison in Belfast because he believed he would be given political status.

However, this request was rejected on the basis that his actions were not political. Campbell's father, Colin, and uncle, William, were jailed for life in 1979 for blowing up two Irish bars in Glasgow which were full of people on a Saturday night. A charge of blowing up a third bar was not proven. Campbell admitted belonging to the proscribed Loyalist terrorist group Ulster Volunteer Force.

This is just one example of sectarian violence in Glasgow. A 2008 article entitled 'Catholics bear the brunt of Scottish sectarian abuse' by Severin Carrell, writing for *The Guardian* on 28 November 2008, stated that sectarian incidents reported to police (largely verbal abuse) increased by 50% to 440 over an eighteen-month period. The article stated that 64% of the 726 cases between 1 January 2004 and 30 June 2005 were motivated by hatred against Catholics, and the remaining percentage was mainly motivated for hatred towards other minority religions.

Rangers' traditional support has largely come, but by no means exclusively, from the Protestant community, while

Celtic's has often, but by no means exclusively, come from those of Irish extraction. The rivalry between the two clubs has often been characterised along sectarian lines. Celtic has had an historic association with the Catholic peoples of Ireland, and some Celtic fans sing Irish Republican songs. Rangers fans are traditionally Loyalists, and most of them sing songs that reflect that point of view. One effect is that Scottish flags are relatively rare among supporters; Celtic fans are more likely to wave the Irish Tricolour while Rangers fans tend to wave the Union flag.

The ferocity of the rivalry has made it rare for a player to represent both teams during his career. Players who have played for both sides of the Old Firm include Alex Bennett, Scott Duncan, Robert Gordon Campbell and George Livingstone, though these players played at a time before the intensity of the rivalry had taken root. Until Graeme Souness signed former Celtic player Mo Johnston in 1989, Rangers were said by him to have had an 'unwritten policy' of not signing any player who was Catholic. Rangers' signing of Johnston caused particular controversy because, although he was not the first Catholic to play for Rangers, he was by far the highest-profile openly Catholic player to do so since World War I. In addition to this, it was the belief of many at Celtic Park that Johnston would re-sign for the club, to the extent that it was publicised that Johnston would be signing. The reasons for the breakdown in Johnston's transfer to Celtic are pure speculation.

Both Rangers and Celtic now accept that they have a problem with sectarianism, and both admit that a proportion of their supporters have been, and continue to be, guilty of perpetuating partisan, sectarian beliefs as well as cultural intolerance. Working alongside the Scottish Parliament, church groups and community organisations such as Nil by Mouth, the Old Firm clubs have clamped down on sectarian songs, inflammatory flag-waving, and troublesome supporters; using increased levels of policing and surveillance. However, disagreements about what constitutes sectarian behavior have undermined progress in these matters, and consensus over what types of songs and flags are acceptable remains difficult to achieve. In 1996, Celtic launched their Bhoys Against Bigotry campaign, later followed by Youth Against Bigotry which, according to then chief executive Ian McLeod, was meant to 'educate the young on having . . . respect for all aspects of the community – all races, all colours, all creeds'. Rangers launched their anti-sectarian campaign, Pride Over Prejudice, in 2003, which has since been renamed, Follow With Pride.

In 2006, Rangers were ordered by UEFA to make a public announcement at all of their home games prohibiting the chanting of the song 'Billy Boys'. Celtic club chairman Brian Quinn dismissed calls to institute a list of what songs are unacceptable at Celtic Park, and chief executive Peter Lawwell defended the singing of 'Irish ballads' at matches.

On 12 April 2006, following an investigation into the conduct of Rangers supporters at both legs of their UEFA Champions League tie against Villarreal CF, the Control and Disciplinary Body of UEFA imposed a fine of £8,800 on Rangers following the improper conduct of some of their supporters, notably the smashing of a window of the Villarreal CF team bus at the second-leg match in Spain on

7 March. However, UEFA declared the Rangers fans not guilty of alleged discriminatory chants.

On 9 June 2006, Rangers, in conjunction with representatives from several supporters clubs, announced that they would comply with three UEFA directives. The club was 'Ordered to announce measurable targets in order to reduce sectarian behaviour amongst its supporters'. The club was 'to control their anti-sectarian activities by producing comprehensive statistics that are communicated to the public'. The club was 'to make a public address announcement at every official fixture, be it international or domestic, stating that any sectarian chanting and any form of the song "Billy Boys" is strictly prohibited'.

Despite these measures, UEFA indicated that they would launch another investigation after Rangers fans clashed with riot police and were filmed making sectarian chants during the defeat by Osasuna in their UEFA Cup match in 2007. The Rangers Supporters Association secretary indicated his belief that a small minority of fans are to blame, suggesting 'it doesn't matter how often they are told to stop sectarian chanting, some people will just not listen'. In September 2007, UEFA praised Rangers for their efforts.

Today, in 2009, sectarianism unfortunately is still alive and kicking in Scotland, when the Rangers fans taunt Celtic supporters and players with the singing of the vile and hideous 'Famine Song'.

The 'Famine Song' has five verses. Here is the first one:

> I often wonder where they would have been
> If we hadn't have taken them in
> Fed them and washed them

THE IDENTITY OF CELTIC

Thousands in Glasgow alone
From Ireland they came
Brought us nothing but trouble and shame
Well the famine is over
Why don't they go home

The Scottish police have advised Rangers that anyone singing this song is in danger of being arrested for a 'racial breach of the peace'.

The Irish government's consulate in Edinburgh was involved in seeking clarification from the Scottish government as to what they were doing about this racist karaoke after letters of complaint had been written to the Irish Embassy in London. So far the official response from the Scottish government has been muted. But the 'Famine Song' is only the most recent manifestation of Scotland's oldest racism – moreover it is tolerated by the leaders of Scottish society. Although Rangers FC are currently subject of a probation order from UEFA for 'discriminatory chanting' during European games, the club will probably escape any sanction from the Scottish soccer authorities for these domestic outpourings of racism towards the Irish community in Scotland by a section of their supporters.

Nowhere in Scotland is more Irish than the east end of Glasgow where Celtic Park proudly stands beneath the Irish Tricolour to remind everyone of the strong link that will always exist between Ireland and Celtic.

8

SODS FROM DONEGAL AND MICHAEL DAVITT

On alien soil like yourself I am here;
I'll take root and flourish of that never fear,
And though I'll be crossed sore and oft by the foes
You'll find me as hardy as Thistle and Rose.
If model is needed on your own pitch you will have it,
Let your play honour me and my friend Michael Davitt.

Here lies a man who from his cradle to his grave was considered by his foes to be a traitor to alien rule and oppression in Ireland and in every land outside her shores.

The epitaph to which Davitt aspired in a speech in the House of Commons, 17 October 1899

Michael Davitt (1846–1906) has been described by American scholar, David Krause, as 'the conscience of Ireland'.

Michael Davitt was born in Straide, Co. Mayo on 25 March 1846. He was the second of five children. When Michael was six years old, his parents, Martin and Sabina Davitt (née Kielty), were evicted during the Great Famine. Martin travelled to find work in England and settled down in Lancashire. His wife and family, refusing shelter in the workhouse, were offered accommodation by the parish priest in Straide, Fr John McHugh.

In 1845 Mrs Davitt and her children joined her husband in the industrial town of Haslingden in Lancashire. In the unlikely environment of the Lancashire mill-town, Martin Davitt earned a reputation as a teacher of both Irish music and the Irish language, so it was only natural that Michael Davitt should grow up speaking Irish.

In 1856, at the age of ten, Michael began work in a cotton mill but two years later had his right arm amputated in an accident. He subsequently attended a Wesleyan school for two years, after which he worked for a printing firm. In 1865, he joined the Irish Republican Brotherhood (IRB) and two years later gave up his job to become organising secretary of the Fenians in Northern England and Scotland. He was arrested in London in 1870 while awaiting a delivery of arms, and was sentenced to fifteen years hard labour. The next seven years were spent in complete isolation in prison, where he was compelled to work in inhuman conditions. With other political prisoners he was released on ticket of leave on 19 December 1877. Michael Davitt subsequently became a member of the Supreme Council of the IRB.

Later he toured America with the active assistance of John Devoy, gaining the support of Irish Americans for his policy which was founded on the slogan 'The Land for the People'. His activities did not have the official approval of the Fenian leadership, many of whom were in fact openly hostile to his methods.

Early in 1879 Davitt returned home to a country which was

once again experiencing near-famine conditions. It was one of the wettest years on record, the potato crop had failed for the third successive year and the traditional escape route of emigration was virtually closed due to a worldwide economic depression stretching from America across England as far as Eastern Europe.

At a large meeting attended by Davitt in Claremorris, County Mayo, plans were made for a huge gathering at Irishtown as part of agitation to reduce rents. The first target was land owned by a Canon Ulick Burke and the result was an astounding success when the Canon was forced to reduce rents by twenty-five per cent. This Irishtown meeting on 20 April 1879 was largely the outcome of organisational work initiated and led by James Daly, Editor of *The Connaught Telegraph*.

On 16 August 1879, the Land League of Mayo was formally founded in Castlebar, County Mayo with the active support of Charles Stewart Parnell. On 21 October 1879 the National Land League was formed in The Imperial Hotel Dublin with Parnell as President and Davitt as one of the secretaries. From that time right on to 1882 the Land War was fought in earnest – British Prime Minister Gladstone at first replied with coercion, but was finally forced into making important concessions.

Davitt would often lend his support and oratorical skills at meetings with the crofters in the Scottish Highlands who were facing the same land problems as in Ireland.

In 1882 Michael Davitt was rearrested. On his release he travelled widely, campaigning ceaselessly for the oppressed everywhere, whether the Boers in South Africa, the Jews in Russia, the working class in Britain or his own people in

Ireland. In 1892 he was elected MP for Mayo but disliked the institution of Parliament and became increasingly impatient with the inability or unwillingness to right injustice.

He left the House of Commons in 1896 with the prophetic prediction that 'No just cause could succeed there unless backed by physical force.'

Davitt died in Dublin in 1906. By the time of his death at the age of sixty, '. . . the land for the people' had largely become a reality, prison reform had begun and he himself had become an international champion of liberty.

To mark the centenary of his birth in 1946 a major demonstration was held in Straide, primarily at the request of a personal friend and executor of his will, Mr Dennis O'Rourke of Dublin. An attendance of over 12,000 included Eamonn de Valera, Hugh Delargy, MP, as well as surviving members of the Davitt family, Dr Robert Davitt and Miss Eileen Davitt. I

When Parkhead was officially opened on 19 March 1892, Celtic officials could think of only one man to perform the task. A sod of Irish turf encrusted with shamrock was taken from Donegal, a county with a strong tradition of immigration to Glasgow. The sense of symbolic decorum and of sanctity almost in Michael Davitt's laying a square of shamrock-encrusted Irish turf on the occasion was tarnished somewhat when a 'midnight gardener' dug up and ran off with the piece of earth. But a poem cursed him for eternity:

The curse of Cromwell blast the hand that stole the sod that Michael cut;
May all his praties turn to sand- the crawling, thieving scut.

That precious site of Irish soil with verdant shamrocks over-
grown
Was token of a glorious soil more fitting far than fretted stone.
Again I say, may Heaven blight that envious, soulless knave;
May all his sunshine be like night and the sod rest heavy on
his grave.

Davitt's connection with Celtic had strong political overtones,
however. Like Celtic, he represented something that was both
native and displaced, that was rooted in a populist Irish nationalism and yet consumed with the social class struggles of
workers, Irish and non-Irish in Ireland, and in the diaspora.
To the Irish in Scotland in particular, Davitt was an intensely
attractive and charismatic man. His Fenian past, the years in
prison and his overcoming of the adversities of eviction, exile
and physical disablement, all combined with his radical agita-
tionary politics to make him a figure of effervescent popularity in Scotland. However, if Davitt was especially
appreciated by the Irish in Scotland through addressing both
their ethnic and social grievances, he, too, found Scotland a
vital arena for the fullest implementation of his pan-Celtic
radicalism.

Thanks to the work of a small committee formed in Straide
thirty years ago, the achievements of Land League founder
Michael Davitt have been given their rightful place in Irish
history. For long a forgotten hero in the annals of Irish history,
Davitt's varied career and achievements are all portrayed
and signposted in the well-appointed Memorial Museum in
his native village. It was a long haul for the dedicated and
enterprising local committee. The association was founded on

9 November 1972 when local woman Nancy Smyth invited a number of people to form a committee. The aim of the committee formed that night was to tidy up Davitt's grave to bring to the attention of his family that the Celtic cross over his grave was slanting and in need of maintenance, and also to see if it would be possible to have the Abbey cleaned as it was then in a very neglected and overgrown state. The newly formed committee operated for two years out of a local house with Michael Howley, RIP, as its first chairman. In May 1974 the committee of nine people decided to enlarge the group with representatives from around the county to become involved.

The aims remained, and are still, the same – to highlight the work of Michael Davitt and to bring tourists to the area. The committee had a strong policy from the beginning that it would operate as a non-political and non-sectarian association. This still holds true. Michael Davitt became known universally as 'The Father of the Land League'. Michael Davitt's last resting place is in the Abbey cloisters about 500 yards from the place where his family were evicted.[19]

For the Rosses Celtic Supporters Club in West Donegal, an event linking them for ever to Celtic Football Club will be a memory which no one involved will ever forget. History had always told us that the original sod at Celtic Park back in 1892 had been given by the famous Irish Land League leader Michael Davitt and that it came from Donegal. The Rosses Celtic Supporters Club felt that it would be a great honour to repeat the deed and to supply a new sod in 1995. It would also be in keeping with the very strong Donegal and Irish connection with Celtic. Within days of the letter being sent,

Fergus McCann, Chairman of Celtic 1994–1999, replied saying that both he and the board would be delighted to receive the first sod for the newly refurbished stadium from Ireland and he gave official permission and the blessing of Celtic to cut a sod of turf in Donegal and transport it to Celtic Park.[20]

Fergus McCann is credited with rescuing the club from imminent bankruptcy; McCann stated at the outset that he would stay for only five years, with the objectives of placing the club on a firmer business footing and returning the league championship to Celtic Park. The latter goal was met, halting Old Firm rivals Rangers FC in their quest for a record-breaking ten consecutive league titles in the season of 1996/97.

On the evening of 10 April 1995, many hundreds gathered at a field in Mullachdubh, in the Rosses, Donegal, to witness the cutting of the sod by members of the Rosses Celtic Supporters Club. In true West Donegal tradition, the local fife and drum bands came out and played a few tunes, RTE News carried the story on the nine o'clock news. The local priest blessed the sod. A sod measuring a yard square was cut and placed on board the bus with fifty supporters and headed off to Glasgow.

Fergus McCann graciously met them at the front door of Celtic Park along with Donegal man Packie Bonner and several Celtic officials together with TV cameras and press. The sod was carried inside the famous main doors and the sense of importance of the day began to hit home. Here were fifty Celtic supporters from the Rosses and Gweedore areas of Donegal carrying 100 years of a Celtic and Irish connection forward for another 100 years.

The ceremony itself was quite simple and many photos

were taken when the sod was put in place in the centre circle underneath the shadow of what was then the steel structure of the new stand. Fergus McCann said a few words about how he felt it was important to keep the great Irish tradition alive and he thanked them for going to the trouble of sourcing and transporting the sod.

9

BELFAST CELTIC 1891–1949

No football club in the history of the game in Ireland has left such a lasting impression in the hearts and minds of people than that of the famous Belfast Celtic. Today, a place exists in the memories of people when, in an era now confined to the history books, The Falls Road in west Belfast was packed with the faithful making their way to 'Paradise', not unlike any home Saturday on the London Road, Glasgow. At the foot of the Donegal Road stands a shopping complex, the Park Centre. For those of another generation it will evoke memories of sadness and loss, for here once stood the famous Celtic Park, for forty-eight glorious years the home of Belfast Celtic Football Club.

As a club it had graced the game for fifty-eight years, opting out finally on St Stephen's Day 1948 when a hooligan Linfield support invaded the pitch at Windsor Park, forcing the Belfast Celtic players from the pitch after a 1–1 draw. The legendary Belfast Celtic was the leading light in Irish soccer from 1891–1949. It had won numerous trophies and was held in high esteem by the sporting community in Ireland and overseas. Despite being forced to withdraw from all competition twice due to political upheaval, the team won the Irish League fourteen times, the Irish Cup eight times, the City Cup ten times and the Gold Cup seven times. But the events of St Stephen's Day 1948 would finally be the end for Belfast Celtic.

The game which ended it for Belfast Celtic was between the top two teams of the period, each from opposite sides of the religious divide in Belfast. Linfield was the established team supported by a people with pro-Unionist sympathies. Belfast Celtic was seen as the team supported by those with pro-Irish or nationalist sympathies. For Belfast's beleaguered Nationalists, Belfast Celtic provided a release from the grim reality of day-to-day life. Bill Cavanaugh once said, 'When we had nothing we had Belfast Celtic, and then we had everything'.

Celtic had been formed in Glasgow in 1887–1888, uniting an Irish population in the east end of the city. The mindset in west Belfast was similar to that of the beleaguered Irish in Glasgow and would yield the same result. In 1891 members of the Milltown club brought into play an idea to form a football team that would be representative of The Falls Road. It was after the Milltown Annual Meeting in the Spring of 1891, held in the old Engineers' Hall, College Street, Belfast, that, after discussing the events of the past season and the chances of Milltown winning the Junior Cup, Frank Laverty, James Keenan and Alec Begley came to the conclusion that had Milltown depended more on local talent, its prospects for success would have been improved. The feeling got about that preference should be given to home talent, knowing that there were a lot of young players about the district who, with a little training, would make first-class players. It was then that they came to the conclusion there should be a single club representative of the Falls. How was it going to be accomplished with any chance of success with other clubs like Milltown on the Falls who had all the support of the district?

The answer was that the players of Clondara and Millvale, a couple of good local juvenile clubs in the area, could be depended upon from which to select a first-class junior team. Frank Laverty, James Keenan and Alec Begley approached Clondara and Millvale with this in mind. The merger was successful and a new team emerged in west Belfast on 14 March 1891. The call for players was sounded with the result that the Millvale boys and the Clondara boys responded. The founding members were: J. Keenan; J. Crummy; D. Reilly; P. McCauley; B. Hayes; H. McArdle; B. Butler; J. Keaney; P. Mooney; A. Begley and F. Laverty.

The club was named after Celtic with the aim of imitating the Scottish-based club in its style of play, following its example in the cause of charity and winning the Irish Cup. James Keenan, after explaining the business of the meeting, which was the formation of a new junior football club thoroughly representative of the Falls, suggested it should be called Belfast Celtic, after its Glasgow friends. His suggestion to call the infant club Belfast Celtic was the only one put forward.

When Belfast Celtic was formed, Bob Hayes, a founding member, was instructed to write to Celtic for assistance. The Glasgow club responded immediately by sending a cheque, much to the surprise of some people, whom it was reported had written warning the Glasgow Celts against sending anything, as the locals could not possibly carry on.

The sum of nine shillings was taken in subscriptions that

night, not much to start a new club with, but sufficient to purchase the first members' cards, which were procured in Doherty's, in Ann Street. It was a hard task disposing of them, as very few took the new club seriously, while many predicted a speedy ending. Some of those who refused to take a member's card at the start became prominent within the club in the following years. Notwithstanding these initial setbacks, the officials and members, in spite of refusals of support from where it was expected, were determined to carry on. The most important business now was to secure a ground, for without one they would surely fail.

At this time one of the Gaelic clubs in the city, Belfast Gaels, was in occupation of a ground at Broadway, which it was considered would be most suitable if terms could be arranged. Frank Laverty and Alec Begley, met the committee of the Belfast Gaels, and as Frank Laverty and the Clondara boys had assisted the Gaels in many of their matches, both in Dublin and most of the towns of the North, it was thought that there would be no difficulty in getting the ground, at least for Saturday evenings.

Eventually the ground was secured for Saturday evenings only, on condition that the full rent of the ground was paid, which, needless to say, was gladly accepted. In fact, any price would have been paid as it was a case of life or death for the club. Having secured the ground, it was decided to apply for admission to a little competition called the Alliance, and it was unanimously admitted. Before the season opened, a friendly match was arranged against a Glentoran eleven, who at that time were considered the best junior team in Ireland. After a hard fought game, in which the young Belfast Celtic gave a good account of themselves, they were only beaten 2–1.

The first Belfast Celtic officials were: James McCann (President); James Keenan (Treasurer); Alec Begley (Secretary); Frank Lavery (Captain) and Harry Laverty (Vice-Captain). The first ground was situated below the Bee Hive, Broadway, Falls Road, on the same side, just where Brighton Street is now, and many hard battles took place on the same pitch.

The Belfast Celtic first team was: J. Hayes; H. Laverty; F. Laverty; J. Cairns; F. Toal; Pat Heaney; W. Cairns; Charley Breen; J. McKenna; P. McAuley and D. Reilly.

Belfast Celtic was admitted into the Irish League in 1896, winning its first championship in 1901. It then moved to its own ground, aptly named Celtic Park, later renamed 'Paradise' which had a capacity of 50,000. The club was controlled by the Barr family with club secretary Bob Barr receiving accreditation for guiding the club through the religious and political circumstances surrounding its formation. Belfast Celtic, unlike city rivals Linfield, was a club like Celtic in Glasgow in that it had a non-sectarian policy in signing players.

It was felt that great progress was made by the young Celts, only 'two years of age', and justified its admission to the Junior League by gaining runners-up position to Distillery II. In the season 1892/93 the team dropped a bombshell in the local football world by beating Cliftonville 2–1 in the semi-final of the County Antrim Shield and in the final were only beaten by Distillery at Grosvenor Park 2–1.

The Robinson & Cleaver Shield had been secured for competition by the League, thanks to the efforts of Frank Osborne (then Secretary of the League) and from the moment that was

announced, Alec Begley and Frank Laverty were determined
to have the name of Belfast Celtic to be the first engraved
upon it – they succeeded. But the winning of the League was
not their only ambition, as again they got to the final of the
County Antrim Shield, only to see Cliftonville reverse the
previous season's defeat in the semi-final and win by 2–1.

The next and last season in the Junior League was the
culminating point of a most consistent effort on the part of
one of the most loyal body of officials and band of players
that ever donned the now famous green and white shirts.
Their record for past seasons will hardly be beaten, by winning
the Junior League three years in succession, in addition to
reaching the final of the Senior Co. Antrim Shield, also three
years in succession, they were undefeated in the Junior League,
having played eighteen matches without a defeat and with
only five goals scored against them. In the final of the Co.
Antrim Shield they met and defeated Distillery by 3–1. This
was a record for a junior team to be in the final of a senior
competition three consecutive seasons out of its first five years
in existence.

When Belfast Celtic was playing so well as a junior club,
it had the determination to challenge Linfield. Having beaten
Distillery, a senior club, in the Antrim Shield final, it felt justified in tackling Linfield. Linfield accepted the challenge across
the divide; the battle took place at the Belfast Celtic pitch at
Broadway. Belfast Celtic won 1–0. In May 1896, the team was
admitted to the Irish Football League. It did not have a pitch
to call home and had to play all its League games on the
ground of its opponents. Still, the club persevered, and a year
later got a pitch at Whiterock Road, familiarly known as

'Klondyke' and afterwards Shaun's Park. Here, the club did a great deal better. In season 1899/1900, Belfast Celtic won the Irish League Championship for the first time, with Linfield runners-up. The Steel Cup final was lost to Cliftonville Olympic 3–0.

In July 1901 Belfast Celtic became a limited company, with a £3,000 capital of £1 shares. The first Board of Directors were: James Millar; John McKenna; David McCloskey; John Rooney; Hugh Fitzpatrick; Charles Watters; Henry Scullion; Patrick McCrush; Hugh McAlinden and Joe Smyth. Celtic Park was acquired. The first League match played at Celtic Park took place on 31 August 1901, against a Glentoran side which, at that time, was at the height of its form. Glentoran won 3–1. The next match was against Ulster at Ballynafeigh and ended in a draw 1–1. The third match was the visit of Derry Celtic. It was the first win at Celtic Park by a score of 2–1.

The first football trophy that came to Celtic Park was the City Cup in the season 1905/06. The competition had finished with Celtic, Linfield and Cliftonville tying for first place. In the resulting test matches Celtic defeated both its rivals. It was retained the following year but five more years elapsed before the club had another football success. This was the Gold Cup, which was won when it was first put up for competition in 1912. The final was played at Grosvenor Park and Glentoran, the favourites, were defeated 2–0. At the conclusion of the season 1911/12, Celtic won the Gold Cup and the Charity Cup, by beating Cliftonville in the final by 3–0 before a record gate of £166. The Seconds won the Steel Cup, beating Glentoran II by 3–1.

At this time in 1912 there was a split in the football governing body; it was now under the jurisdiction of a body styled 'The New Football Association of Ireland'. During the summer of this year there was an adjustment of the football dispute, but the season 1912/13 opened with the IFA in control.

An Irish Cup tie in season 1912/13 against Bohemians at Celtic Park brought crisis for Belfast Celtic, which almost culminated in its exit from football. Neal Clarke of Belfast Celtic was sent off and an amazed and unhappy home support invaded the pitch. The referee's decisions did not go down well with the crowd. However, the referee's (Mr Entwistle) report was an eye-opener to the Belfast Celtic officials, as he blamed the whole thing on Neal Clarke for having, it was alleged, kicked an opponent, an incident actually witnessed by very few. The IFA, after a lengthy sitting, came to the conclusion at two o'clock in the morning that Clarke would be suspended for ten months and that the ground be closed for one month. The only people who openly protested against the injustice of the sentence were Jimmy Clarke, of Cliftonville and Frank Toal, who bluntly told the Committee that the punishment was harsh and unjustifiable.

The Belfast Celtic following took the IFA decision badly. It was the eve of the County Antrim Shield semi-final against Linfield at Grosvenor Park and it was felt by many this would be Belfast Celtic's farewell to football. As a result of Neal Clarke's suspension, Andy Davison was brought in to fill the centre forward position. Fortune would smile on a dismayed Belfast Celtic. Davison scored a hat-trick and turned what looked like a defeat into a resounding 3–2 victory. It was a major factor in deciding that Belfast Celtic would not go out of football; as the team went on to win the Shield, beating Glentoran in the final by 3–1 at Cliftonville.

In September 1912 there occurred an infamous riot at Celtic Park. It was at a League match versus Linfield and, as the trouble began during the interval without any preliminaries or formal declaration of war, the teams and officials were in blissful ignorance of the outbreak until it was well under way. The game was not resumed and was replayed peacefully in mid-week a month later.

A continental tour was arranged to Prague in the month of June, 1912. Altogether there were six matches played, the Belfast Celts winning five and drawing one. Harry Buckle did most of the scoring. In the drawn match, the referee never moved from the corner flag during the whole game.

In the season 1914/15 the League Championship was won for the second time, and the first since Celtic Park became club headquarters. The team dropped out of senior football between 1915 and 1917 but continued to have major success at junior level.

Belfast Celtic left senior football again in 1920 after a man in the crowd at a cup semi final produced a revolver and fired shots into the crowd. This took place during the Irish War of Independence and when the Black and Tans opened fire on Gaelic football players and spectators in Croke Park in a similar occurrence. The club was persuaded back into senior football in 1924 to ease the existing political unrest. The return of Belfast Celtic marked a glorious era, winning ten League Championships in sixteen years.

It is most remarkable that all the record gates in charity matches have been made when Belfast Celtic played. Year after year, the receipts increased until the team's last season when they went well into four figures. In this respect Belfast Celtic were certainly upholding the motto of their big brothers, Celtic in Glasgow.

It was in March 1920 that a crowd disturbance occurred at the Cliftonville grounds at an Irish Cup semi-final between Belfast Celtic and Glentoran which led to the club taking legal action against the decision of the IFA. The club was to be fined and suspended over the matter. The action was settled out of court culminating in the IFA withdrawing its decision and paying all costs. Political upheaval caused the club to abandon all competition from the beginning of the season 1920/21 till season 1924/25. Austin Donnelly, the then chairman of the company, formed a team of local juniors, who gave a highly creditable display in the Senior League, finishing third in the table. This team formed the nucleus of the all-conquering team of 1925/26, which won all the senior competitions with the exception of the County Antrim Shield and, by defeating the Free State champions in Dublin, was entitled to an All-Ireland title.

Beginning with season 1925/26, the League Championship was won four years in succession, a feat not previously accomplished by any other Irish club, though it was subsequently repeated by the team once more. The performance of 1928/29 was perhaps the greatest performance in Irish football; a League score of 116 goals with twenty-three against and a total of forty-eight points out of a possible fifty-two and an undefeated record in the season which has no parallel.

Belfast's version of the 'Old Firm' attracted sell-out crowds, but the sectarian and politically unstable nature of post-World

War I Irish society ensured that Belfast Celtic fans were literally marked out as targets:

> Anyone showing visible support for the club would be assumed to be a Catholic and could, unknowingly, have their coat marked with chalk. As they made their way home through the infamous Dee Street that led from the Oval (Glentoran's ground), they would be set upon by Protestant adversaries.[21]

Such common episodes of violence during a time of Civil War in Ireland led Belfast Celtic to quit the league in 1920, unable to guarantee the safety of officials or fans. They left as champions and returned four years later to embark upon a run of incredible success, winning the title in the Wartime Regional League fifteen times between 1925 and 1948.

Another glorious season was 1926/27, winning the Irish League (without a defeat) for the second year in succession, also the County Antrim Shield, beating Dunmurry, the well-known Intermediate team, by 3–2. 1927/28 was marked by the third successive win of the League Championship, thus falling into line with Linfield, the only other team to have won the League three times in succession (which they did on two occasions), also the City Cup. The season 1928/29 will be remembered for the second greatest event in the history of the club and the greatest in the history of the Irish League competition, when the League Championship was won for the fourth season in succession, a feat never before accomplished by any other club.

The defining moment in the history of Belfast Celtic came with the 1948 St Stephen's Day meeting of Belfast Celtic and

Linfield at Windsor Park. Two Linfield players were carried off, one from each side sent off, a late Belfast Celtic penalty and an even later equaliser for eight-man Linfield proved too much for the home fans, who invaded the pitch at full-time. They attacked the Belfast Celtic players, breaking the leg of Jimmy Jones while the RUC looked on, unable or unwilling to intervene.

It was the final straw for the club's directors. Within four months they had sold off their most valuable assets – including Ireland international Bud Aherne to Luton – and thrown in the towel. Jones was once on Linfield's books but was not rated highly enough to be given a contract. He left to join Belfast Celtic, where he became an instant hit. He was then approached by the Linfield secretary Joe Mackey, who tried to get him to leave 'those Taigs' and come back to his 'natural' home. Jones, a Protestant, was disgusted and gave the official short shrift, a response that was to have grave repercussions during the St Stephen's Day encounter. An innocuous challenge involving the winger and Linfield's Bob Bryson resulted in the latter being carried off with a leg injury. Little wonder, then, that the Belfast Celtic man found himself the chief target during the ensuing violence. He was lucky, to a certain extent, in that a double-fracture did not stop him from resuming his career. The club had no such reprieve. Perhaps the directors planned a temporary exile, as had happened in 1920, but the conditions for a return were never quite right and, come the civil rights protests of the 1960s, there was no way such an overtly Catholic and nationalist sporting body could have survived the social upheaval.

As if Belfast Celtic hadn't damaged enough reputations in

its time, the greatest upset of all occurred on 29 May 1949 when it faced the then home international champions, Scotland, at the Tribro Stadium. Soccer history was made and recorded forever when Belfast Celtic defeated the Scottish 'wonder team' by 2–0. Two days previously Belfast Celtic had been replaced in the league by Crusaders and, given the traumatic events of the previous season, it is remarkable that this club side defeated any national side, let alone the British champions. It was a feat never to be repeated. The last time Belfast Celtic graced 'Paradise' was 17 May 1952 when it played Jimmy McGrory's Celtic in a charity match. On show that day were Jock Stein, Sean Fallon and Charlie Tully, who played for Celtic.

'Paradise' continued to function as a greyhound stadium until the 1980s when it was bulldozed and replaced by a shopping centre. Today, a small plaque reminds shoppers of the glory days.

The rivalry between Belfast Celtic and Linfield was the strength behind the league and without it the league suffered. West Belfast was left without a major football team until the formation of Donegal Celtic in 1970. The city of Belfast never recovered from the loss of Belfast Celtic and neither did Irish football. The formation in 2003 of the Belfast Celtic Society is living proof that the Grand Old Team is not forgotten.

Irish League Championship
1899/1900, 1914/15, 1919/20, 1925/26, 1926/27, 1927/28, 1928/29, 1932/33, 1935/36, 1936/37 1937/38, 1938/39, 1939/40, 1940/41
1941/42 Regional League Championship.
1943/44 Regional League Championship.

James Grant

John Glass

Brother Walfrid

John O'Hara

John McLaughlin

Celtic Football Club 1889

Tom Maley Brake Club,
Glasgow, 1892

St. Mary's Hall in Calton, Glasgow where Celtic
Football Club was formed 6th November 1887

CELTICS FIRST SOD OF TURF
IT WAS IN THIS FIELD ON THE 10TH
DAY OF APRIL 1995 THAT THE FIRST
SOD OF TURF FOR THE NEW CELTIC
PARK IN GLASGOW WAS CUT

THIS COMMEMORATION STONE WAS
LATER UNVEILED BY GLASGOW CELTIC
CAPTAIN PAUL McSTAY ON THE 2ND
DAY OF JUNE 1995

Plaque to the
sod of turf cut
in Donegal 1995
by the Rosses CSC
and planted in
Celtic Park

Celtic Football Club 1908.
Back row: T. White,
J. Kelly, T. Colgan,
J. McKillop, J. Grant,
M. Dunbar;
middle row: W. Maley
(manager), J. Young,
P. Somers, J. McMenemy,
D. Adams, J. Mitchell,
J. Weir, R. Davis (trainer);
front row: D. Hamilton,
D. McLeod, W. Loney,
J. Hay, J. Quinn,
A. McNair

Celtic legend Patsy
Gallacher, 1925

Patsy Gallacher in action for Celtic 1912

Plaque in memory of Patsy Gallacher on the
wall of his home in Ramelton, Co. Donegal

Brian and Colin McGuirk with
the European Cup

BROTHER WALFRID

Statue of Brother Walfrid, born in
Ballymote, Co. Sligo on 18 May 1840.
This statue was solely funded by
Celtic supporters and unveiled outside
Celtic Park on 5 November 2005.

Author Brian McGuirk with the European
Cup at a CSC function, Dundalk, 1999

Back row: Michael Kelly, Jim Greenan, Dixie Dean, Joe McBride, Evan Williams, Jim Kelly, Shane Fox;
front row: Darren O'Dea, Michael MacDonald, Tom Maher, Sean Fallon, Aisling Kane, Paul Hartley

Aiden McGeady with AICSC Chairman Tom Maher

Aiden McGeady and Darren O'Dea with the SPL trophy

Neil Lennon, Marie Maher, Tom Maher and Stephen McManus

Tom Maher,
Stephen McManus,
Aiden McGeady,
Paddy McCourt,
Darren O'Dea,
Andreas Hinkel
and Neil Lennon

Celtic players and staff and AICSC Committee with
the SPL trophy

Neil Lennon speaking at the AICSC
Dinner Dance in the City West
Hotel, Dublin

Sean Fallon in a Celtic sing song in Dublin. Tom Maher, AICSC Chairman, in centre

Celtic Park, Glasgow

Tony Slack of Tanzy Burns CSC, West Belfast, at the funeral of Celtic legend Jimmy Johnstone, 17 March 2006

Above and right:
A great supporters'
tribute to former
Celtic player and
manager, Tommy
Burns, outside Celtic
Park May 2008

Caolan, Tony, Róisin
and John Slack of
Tanzy Burns CSC,
Belfast, at the home
of the Orlando CSC
in USA

Members of Tanzy Burns CSC
in Las Vegas

Shane Fox, Jim Greenan, Ken Slattery, Jim Kelly,
Michael Kelly, Tom Maher and Jim Gallagher at
AICSC meeting in Tullamore, Co. Offaly

Gerry McDonnell,
Tom Maher and
Gus MacNamara at
AICSC meeting

Tony Slack and Dan Sloan at
Estádio Nacional, Lisbon, where
Celtic won the European Cup on
25 May 1967

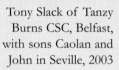

Tony Slack of Tanzy
Burns CSC, Belfast,
with sons Caolan and
John in Seville, 2003

Tony Slack with Lisa McIlroy and Angela Brady of
Eire go Bragh CSC in Bordeaux 2003

Members of Tanzy Burns CSC on their
travels with Bordeaux supporters, 2003

BELFAST CELTIC 1891–1949

1946/47 Regional League Championship.
1947/48 Regional League Championship.

Irish Challenge Cup
1917/18, 1925/26, 1936/37, 1937/38, 1940/41, 1942/43,
1943/44, 1946/47

Irish Gold Cup
1911/12, 1925/26, 1934/35, 1938/39, 1939/40
1940/41 Regional Gold Cup.
1943/44 Regional Gold Cup.
1945/46 Regional Gold Cup.
1946/47 Regional Gold Cup.
1947/48 Regional Gold Cup.

Belfast City Cup
1905/06, 1906/07, 1925/26, 1927/28, 1929/30, 1930/31,
1932/33, 1939/40, 1947/48, 1948/49

County Antrim Shield
1894/95, 1909/10, 1926/27, 1935/36, 1936/37, 1938/39,
1942/43, 1944/45

Belfast Celtic was created in the image of Celtic and from that city every week thousands of the faithful leave on ferries that take them across the water to pay homage in Celtic Park to strengthen the link that will always exist between Ireland and Celtic.

10

FIELDS OF ATHENRY
(AND OTHER CELTIC SONGS)

Fields of Athenry

By a lonely prison wall
I heard a young girl calling
Michael they are taking you away
For you stole Trevelyn's corn
So the young might see the morn
Now a prison ship lies waiting in the bay

Chorus
Low lie the fields of Athenry
Where once we watched the small free birds fly
Our love was on the wing
We had dreams and songs to sing
It's so lonely round the fields of Athenry

By a lonely prison wall
I heard a young man calling
Nothing matters Mary when you're free
Against the famine and the crown

FIELDS OF ATHENRY

I rebelled they ran me down
Now you must raise our child with dignity

[Chorus]

By a lonely harbour wall
She watched the last star falling
As the prison ship sailed out against the sky
Sure she'll wait and hope and pray
For her love in Botany Bay
It's so lonely round the fields of Athenry

[Chorus]

On 27 August 1994, goals from John Collins and Paul McStay gave Celtic a 2–0 victory in Tommy Burns' first Old Firm match as manager.

That day was also memorable for the fact it was the first time the legendary song the 'Fields of Athenry' was sung at a game collectively by the Celtic support. The old usual repertoire of songs was being belted out by both set of supporters. When the Rangers fans in the enclosure sang a song for which the words were not recognisable but the tune was, it was not long before the Broomloan Road Stand erupted with the now famous chorus and a new song was born into the Celtic folklore.

'Fields of Athenry' is a song about the Irish Potato Famine, composed in 1979 by Inchicore (Co. Dublin) songwriter Pete St John. Widely seen as the definitive folk song on the Irish Famine, 'Fields of Athenry' tells the story of the famine through the personal experiences of someone jailed and deported to Australia.

The song, which was first recorded by Irish ballad singer Paddy Reilly, recounts the tale of a fictional Irishman in prison, reporting the story he could hear through the prison walls of another prisoner who was being deported to Botany Bay for stealing food to feed his starving family. The Trevelyn mentioned in the line 'For you stole Trevelyn's corn' was a factual character. His role in the Irish Famine is explained in chapter one.

The claim has been made that the words originate from a broadsheet ballad published in the 1880s by Devlin in Dublin with a different tune. However, there does not appear to have been a publisher called 'Devlin' in Dublin and no copy of such a broadsheet is known to exist. Pete St John has stated definitively that he wrote the words as well as the music, so the story of the 1880s broadsheet may be false.

Athenry (*Baile Átha an Rí* – Ford of the Kings – in Irish Gaelic) is an agricultural town in County Galway in the Republic of Ireland. It lies 25 km to the east of Galway city. One of the attractions of the town is its medieval castle. The town derives its name from the fact that a ford (*Áth*) crossed the river Clare just east of the settlement. Because three kingdoms met at that point, it was called *Áth an Rí*, or *the Ford of the Kings (Kingdoms)*. On some medieval maps of English origin the town is called Kingstown. The kingdoms were Hy-Many to the north-east, east and south-east; Aidne to the south and south-west; Maigh-Seola to the west and north-west. However, there is no historical evidence of any kings being associated with the town, despite its name.

FIELDS OF ATHENRY

The first battle of Athenry was fought on 15 August 1249. Athenry had existed as a minor settlement prior to its foundation as a town by the de Bermingham family in 1241 and was thus still little more than a military base in highly hostile territory.

The victor of the day was Jordan de Exeter, Sheriff of Connacht.

The second battle of Athenry took place on 10 August 1316 and was one of the most decisive battles of the Bruce Wars. It was in many ways part of a war within a war, as Felim mac Aedh Ua Conchobair wished to make himself Supreme King of Connacht, without opposition, and to expel the Normans to regain the lands and power that his family had enjoyed prior to their arrival in 1232. He gathered an impressive array of allies – the Kings of Thomond, Breifne, Moylurg, Hy-Many – in addition to over a dozen lesser kings and lords from Connacht and its borders (Annaly, Leney, Ui Fiachrach Muaidhe, Munster), as well as the probable assistance of Scots gallowglasses.

They were opposed by the Normans of Connaught and their two most prominent leaders; Richard Og de Burgh, Second Earl of Ulster, and Piers de Bermingham, Lord of Athenry. They were aided by lesser Norman lords from all over Connacht and Thomond, as well as some Irish allies.

The collective number of both armies is unknown and can only be estimated. While it is doubtful that the numbers were any higher than 7,000, and even this figure should be treated with caution, the list of participants on the Irish side alone indicates that an overall figure of at least 3,000–4,000 were involved. For much of its history the town of Athenry was safe behind its walls, erected in the aftermath of the second battle of Athenry in 1316 during the height of the Bruce Wars. However, the beginning of the end occurred during the Mac an Iarla Wars in 1572. This was the first of a number of attacks committed by the Mac an Iarlas, and later, by Red Hugh O'Donnell. By the end of the sixteenth century Athenry, once the premier town in Connacht, was reduced to a shell, and did not begin to truly recover till the late 1990s.

The singing of the 'Fields of Athenry' by the Celtic support at Celtic Park is something to be experienced. This folk song is recognition by the Celtic support that they do indeed 'know their history' – a proud history that links Ireland to Celtic forever.

Other songs that are sung, mostly at away games due to song restrictions at Celtic Park, include 'This Land is Your Land', which is an adaptation of the original written by the American folk musician Woody Guthrie in 1940 and recorded by Celtic-orientated bands Charlie and the Bhoys, Saoirse and Shebeen. Other songs are 'Let the People Sing' and 'Bring Them Home'.

This Land is Your Land

This land is your land,
This land is my land
From the northern highlands,
To the western islands.
From the hills of Kerry,
To the streets of Free Derry,
This land was made for you and me.

As I went walking, by the Shannon waters
Hand in hand with my little daughter

FIELDS OF ATHENRY

Hear the church bells ringing
And the children singing
This land was made for you and me.

This land is your land,
This land is my land
From the northern highlands,
To the western islands.
From the hills of Kerry,
To the streets of Free Derry,
This land was made for you and me.

I climbed the mountain
By the crystal fountains
And I heard a great roar
From the rocky seashore.
Her eyes were gleaming,
She said 'Oh daddy'
This land was made for you and me.

This land is your land,
This land is my land
From the northern highlands,
To the western islands.
From the hills of Kerry,
To the streets of Free Derry,
This land was made for you and me.

I walked her home by
The old church steeple

CELTIC FC – THE IRELAND CONNECTION

Proud of my country
Proud of my people
From the men who cried there
To the men who died there singing that
This land was made for you and me.

This land is your land,
This land is my land
From the northern highlands,
To the western islands.
From the hills of Kerry,
To the streets of Free Derry,
This land was made for you and me.

Let the People Sing

For those who are in love
There's a song that's warm and tender.
For those who are oppressed
In song you can protest
So liberate your minds
And give your soul expression.
Open up your hearts,
I'll sing for you this song.

Let the people sing their stories and their songs
And the music of their native land
Their lullabies and battlecries and songs of hope and joy
So join us hand in hand
All across this ancient land

FIELDS OF ATHENRY

Throughout the test of time
It was music that kept their spirits free
Those songs of yours and of mine.
It was back in ancient times,
The bard would tell his stories
Of the heroes, of the villain,
Of the chieftains in the glen.
Through Elizabethan time
And Cromwellian war and fury
Put our pipers to the sword,
Killed our harpers and our bards.

Let the people sing their stories and their songs
And the music of their native land
Their lullabies and battlecries and songs of hope and joy
So join us hand in hand
All across this ancient land
Throughout the test of time
It was music that kept their spirits free
Those songs of yours and of mine.

Ireland, land of song,
Your music lives forever
In its valleys, in its mountains,
In its hills and in its glens.
Our music did survive
Through famine and oppression.
To the generations gone,
I'll sing for you this song.

CELTIC FC – THE IRELAND CONNECTION

Let the people sing their stories and their songs
And the music of their native land
Their lullabies and battlecries and songs of hope and joy
So join us hand in hand
All across this ancient land
Throughout the test of time
It was music that kept their spirits free
Those songs of yours and of mine.

Bring Them Home

Hear it ring on the air
It's the voice of my country so fair
Can't you feel can't you see
Irishmen will set them free
In the jail that held McSweeney
In the prison where he died
Lies two daughters of old Ireland
And they fill my heart with pride
For I know that England wishes
That we'd let them die alone
But the voice of dear old Ireland
Cries for us to bring them home
Hear it ring on the air
It's the voice of my country so fair
Can't you feel can't you see
Irishmen will set them free
Twas the love of dear old Ireland
Brought them to a prison hell
But the ghosts of Pearse and Connolly

FIELDS OF ATHENRY

Filled their lonely prison cell
Clarke and Plunkett stand beside them
McDonagh, McDermott and Wolfe Tone
And all the voices of old Ireland
Cry for us to bring them home
Hear it ring on the air
It's the voice of my country so fair
Can't you feel can't you see
Irishmen will set them free
So I pray you men of Ireland
Don't betray our daughters true
Proudly stand beside our heroes
Lest they die for me and you
Though the tyrant would deny us
We can break their hearts of stone
And all of Ireland will be singing
When we bring our daughters home.

The above songs are sung by the Celtic Support in recognition of the hardship their forefathers had faced back in Ireland and in triumph to the foundation of the football club and tradition that is now Celtic.

11

WHY WE SUPPORT CELTIC

The idea behind this book stemmed from a statement in the Irish printed media as described in the Introduction. The rhetorical question was asked by the journalist: 'why do we (the Irish and our diaspora) support a team that plays its football in Scotland?'

What I wanted to do from the very outset was to revoke this question and clearly state in printed words that this is 'why we support a team that plays its football in Scotland'. Like all Celtic supporters I do know my history on the formation of Celtic Football Club. Almost every person being Irish, or being of Irish descent, has a special place in their hearts for Celtic. The story of Celtic from its humble beginnings is one that has passed down generations. The flame that was ignited by Brother Walfrid is still very much burning within the Celtic support in Ireland and around the world with the various supporters clubs bodies that now exist. Celtic is much more than a football club; Celtic is an identity – an identity that will always link Ireland to the east end of Glasgow and to Celtic forever.

When Ireland was suffering the horrors of the Famine, Irish

people took the boats to Glasgow in search of a better life. They faced the same adversity there as they had in Ireland. They needed a guiding figure to ease the suffering. Brother Walfrid from Sligo, along with John Glass and Pat Welsh amongst others, were such men. Celtic was formed in 1887/88. The Irish Tricolour proudly flies over Celtic Park as a testimony of the roots of the club. Michael Davitt from County Mayo planted the first sod of turf in the current Celtic Park, a sod taken from County Donegal. Willie Maley, Celtic's longest serving manager and the most successful, was from Newry in County Down. So far fifty or so men of Irish birth have played for Celtic down through the years. The song we sing in Celtic Park, 'Fields of Athenry', is a town in County Galway. Belfast Celtic was a team created in the image of Celtic, and is a team still talked about today with respect.

Thousands of Irish travel every week from Ireland to watch Celtic play and to join the diaspora in the east end of Glasgow. Why do they do this? Why do they leave Ireland every weekend to watch a football team play its football in Scotland? The answer is very simple; they all 'know their history'.

I hope you have enjoyed reading this as much as I have enjoyed researching and writing it. It has indeed been a journey for me and, as all journeys go, there has to be an end. I hope the end for me is that I have shown beyond contradiction that this is why 'we support a team that plays its football in Scotland'.

APPENDIX I

PLAYERS AND STAFF FROM IRELAND AND OF IRISH DESCENT

Ireland, through its direct association, has provided Celtic with players, managers and coaching staff of Irish birth and Irish descent since its very inception. From Willie Maley, born in Newry, Co. Down who featured in the first ever Celtic team in 1888 and who went on to the position of manager for forty-three years, to William Flood, born in Dublin, Irish men have proudly worn the stripes (Celtic wore stripes until 1903) and the hoops over the decades. Here each Celtic player, manager and member of the coaching staff of Irish birth and Irish descent is profiled down through the years.

PLAYERS AND STAFF FROM IRELAND

Willie Maley
William Patrick Maley was born in Newry, Co. Down, Ireland on 25 April 1868. He was the first manager of Celtic Football Club and one of the most successful managers in the history of

Scottish football. Under his guidance Celtic won thirty major trophies in his forty-three year tenure as manager at Celtic Park. As a young man he was more involved in athletics than football, although he had played for Cathcart Hazelbank Juniors in 1886 and also Third Lanark, an army team, possibly from the fact his father had been a sergeant in the British Army while living in Newry. In 1888, he was signed by the newly formed Celtic and became one of the new club's first players, as a midfielder. As a naturalised Scot, he also played for the Scottish national team. In 1896, he made a single appearance for Manchester City in a Second Division match against Loughborough. In 1897, the board of Celtic directors appointed Willie Maley, at just twenty-nine years of age, as Secretary-Manager – the first manager – of Celtic. He won the League Championship for the club in his first full season as manager. Willie Maley was and still is the longest serving manager at Celtic. In his forty-three years as manager, he won sixteen league titles, fourteen Scottish Cups, fourteen Glasgow Cups and nineteen Glasgow Charity Cups. The Maley years at Celtic Park ended in a less than amicable fashion. With Celtic at the bottom of the table, after a meeting with the board of directors in February 1940, Willie Maley retired. William 'Willie' Maley died in Glasgow on 2 April 1958. His Celtic career is detailed in song, 'Willie Maley' by David Cameron, and is one of the most popular Celtic songs amongst the Celtic support (see chapter five).

Thomas Morrison

Thomas 'Ching' Morrison was the youngest of five sons born to James and Annie Morrison. The first three boys were born in Scotland and the youngest of them, Bob, who was also an international, played for Linfield until his untimely death from pneumonia in 1891, aged just twenty-three. Another brother, Alex, also played for Glentoran in the 1890s. Thomas was born in Belfast in 1874. He made his first appearance for Glentoran on 18 April 1891 in a Charity Cup game against Ulster at Solitude. He scored in that match, which was abandoned with Glentoran trailing 4–1. The following season (1891/92) saw 'Ching' score eleven goals in just nine games, including a hat-trick in the Irish League against Ligoneil.

Morrison was part of Glentoran's Irish League winning side of 1893/94 and in March of that season he moved to Burnley. He scored on his Burnley debut, a 3–1 victory against Derby County, but early the following season he was dismissed by the Burnley committee for 'misconduct'. He returned to Glentoran and at the end of the 1894/95 campaign he was capped against England, Wales and Scotland. In that final game against Scotland in Glasgow he gave Dan Doyle (fullback) such a torrid time that Willie Maley signed him for Celtic. He made his first team debut on 27 April 1895 in a 2–0 victory over Clyde. That match saw Morrison appear as a trialist and it was not until after the game that he signed officially for the club. He scored for Celtic in the Glasgow Merchant's Charity Cup final, in which Celtic defeated Rangers 4–0 at Cathkin Park on 25 May 1895. Thomas Morrison returned to Burnley in February 1897 and helped them to the Second Division title in 1898. He won four further caps before joining Manchester United in 1902/03. He remained there until the beginning of the 1904/05 season when he signed for Colne. Thomas Morrison returned home to Belfast and ended his career with Glentoran, scoring two goals in sixteen appearances in 1906/07. Thomas Morrison died on 26 March 1940 in Belfast.

Pat Farrell

Pat Farrell came from Belfast. His football career started with Ligoneil before he joined the famous Belfast Celtic in 1894 and Distillery the following year. He won an Irish Cup medal with Distillery in 1896 and his style of play was described as 'merely useful'. He signed for Celtic on 1 August 1896. With many of the Celtic stars of the day on strike due to wage restrictions Farrell was added to the depleted Celtic side to face Arthurlie in the first round of the Scottish Cup at Barrhead on 9 January 1897. Celtic started the game with seven players. With the odds hugely stacked against them, they went crashing out 4–2. This was his only appearance for Celtic. On 4 May 1897 he joined Arsenal before joining Brighton United the following year. The best part of his career came in 1900 when he began his second spell with Distillery. He was capped twice against Scotland and Wales in 1901. He finally joined the team of Brighton and Hove Albion on 31 July 1901 until he hung up his boots in 1904.

John Blair

John Blair was born in Belfast. His football career started at Cliftonville in April 1904. He then moved to Belfast Celtic in January 1908. When he moved to Glasgow to work in the shipyards at Clydebank, Celtic snapped him up in October

1910. He played only one game against Third Lanark in a 0–0 draw on 19 November 1910, in a forward line reading Blair, McMenemy, Quinn, Johnstone and Kivlichan. Had he been a left winger, or a halfback or a back, he would perhaps, have been of more value to Celtic. He failed to make enough of an impact but went on to play six times for Motherwell, for whom he signed in December 1910. He moved back to Belfast to play for Belfast Celtic in 1911, Linfield 1912, Shelbourne (Dublin) 1912, Cliftonville 1914 before retiring in 1915.

Patsy Gallacher

There are few players in the history of Celtic so fondly recalled as the great Patsy Gallacher. Born in the Milford workhouse Co. Donegal on 16 March 1891 to Willie and Margaret, both of whom were illiterate, Patsy Gallacher was one of a family of seven children, four boys and three girls. Willie worked in Ramelton as a mail van driver but found it a continuous struggle to support such a large family. Towards the end of the nineteenth century, in a country rampant with poverty and depression, the Gallachers left their native Donegal and emigrated to Scotland in search of a better and more sustainable life. The family settled in Clydebank at number 32 John Knox Street.

It was here that the 'Gallacher' name was about to change. The man who came to put up the postal nameplate on the door spelt the name as 'Gallagher' in error but the family decided to leave it, as the Scottish spelling might give them more credibility when searching for work.

Willie found employment almost immediately as a ship-yard storeman and the young Patsy attended the local Holy Redeemer primary school. At the age of fifteen he left school to start a five-year apprenticeship as a carpenter in the John Brown shipyard. During this time, in 1907, at the age of sixteen, Patsy was playing with a juvenile team called Renfrew St James, a very successful local side.

By now the family had settled into a very different lifestyle in Clydebank, work was plentiful and, while the wages weren't massive, it was a totally different environment from the one they had left behind in Ireland. Were it not for the Gallacher parents' decision to relocate to the West of Scotland, we might never have heard of the prowess of Patsy Gallacher on the football field.

Patsy was slight in physical attributes, weighing in at less than nine stones and only some five foot five inches in height. He was, however, naturally fit and Willie Maley allowed him the take it or leave it option when it came to training. More often than not Patsy would leave it. Maley viewed training as exercise for those who needed to keep their weight down and as this didn't apply to Patsy, he was happy if Patsy didn't move a muscle from one game to the next.

Because of his slight build and frame, most of the senior clubs failed to show any interest in Patsy. He was deemed as unsuitable to the more physical game, which was prevalent at the time. However, it was Clydebank Juniors which gave him the chance to try his luck. He played there throughout season 1910/11. It was at this time that the young Ramelton lad was brought to the attention of Willie Maley by John Dunlop, a soccer writer for the *Daily Record*. While Patsy was starring for Clydebank, Celtic, by its own standards, was in a dismal state. It was time to explore new talents. Maley was soon to attend a Clydebank match and see Patsy Gallacher for himself. The Gallacher era was about to begin.

'If you put that wee thing out on the park, you'll be done for manslaughter!' Jimmy Quinn said to Celtic manager Willie Maley after first seeing Patsy Gallacher.

In October 1911 Celtic and Clydebank were to play in their traditional friendly and Patsy was given the option to turn out for either side. He chose Celtic. Having scored twice in that game, a month later Patsy was invited to play again in a friendly against an army team. He scored a hat-trick.

The Celtic directors were summoned on the matter of obtaining Patsy Gallacher's signature. As Patsy had yet to complete his apprenticeship as a shipwright, it was decided by all concerned that he would firstly complete this and then join Glasgow Celtic. On 25 October 1911, Patsy Gallacher, at the age of twenty, became a Celtic player. The glorious years of the six in a row had come to an end and, despite winning the Scottish Cup, beating Hamilton Academicals 2–0 after a replay, it was the right time for new talent to join the team. After a successful run in the reserves, Patsy made his debut at Celtic Park against St Mirren on Sunday, 11 December 1911. While not a great performance, he did enough to secure a place on the senior team.

Patsy was included in the team to face Hearts in the Scottish Cup semi-final of 1912. At the tender age of twenty-one, Gallacher was to come of age in front of 45,000 fans when Celtic faced Clyde in the final at Ibrox. Celtic won 2–0 with Patsy scoring the second goal.

Having won his first senior medal with Celtic, it would not be until 1914 until he received his first championship medal. With war in Europe having an impact on everyone, sport too began to feel its tightening grip. Wages were drastically reduced and after only one full season as a player, Patsy returned to carpentry at John Brown's shipyard to supplement his wages. Celtic won the league again in 1915, which would culminate in a four in a row in 1917.

The Scottish Cup final of 1924/25 was the stage for possibly the greatest ever goal seen in Hampden. Taking control of the ball just inside the Dundee half, Patsy rode challenge after challenge until a last gasp tackle finally brought him to the ground inside the six yard box. He was grounded for an instant but with the ball still between his feet. A quick somersault saw him and the ball end up in the Dundee net.

In the summer of 1925 Patsy travelled to the United States to play a series of friendly games at the age of thirty-four. By now Patsy was plagued by injury and his Celtic demise was brought forward by another knee injury. His final goal for his beloved Celtic came against Rangers on 7 October 1925 in a Glasgow Cup semi-final. In season 1926/27, after fifteen years at Celtic Park, it was time for the departure of Patsy Gallacher. Willie Maley had remarked in the club year-book 'that Patsy Gallacher had retired', but Patsy insisted he was as fit as a fiddle. Following a benefit match for Jimmy Quinn on 18 August he met with club directors in Maleys Bank restaurant to discuss signing for one more year. They were not convinced by his fitness claim and a minimum wage was the only offer made. When Patsy refused, he was made available for transfer. Falkirk bought him for £1,500, where he played until 1932 aged forty-one, so proving the Celtic board wrong.

He had married his sweetheart Mary Josie Donegan from Renfrew on 28 June 1915 and together they ran a small tobacconist's shop. On 29 June 1919 she gave birth to a son, William, who in years to come would also don the hoops of Glasgow Celtic. Patsy also ran a very successful pub in Clydebank. In 1929, after giving birth to their sixth child, Mary developed complications and died on 30 June. This tragedy understandably had a huge effect on Patsy. He developed cancer sometime around 1950 and, despite many operations and treatment, he sadly passed away on 17 June 1953. He was sixty-two.

The 'Mighty Atom', so called because of his diminutive stature, weighing less than nine stones and only five foot five inches in height and his incredible work rate, made 464 appearances for Celtic, scoring 192 goals in a career that spanned fifteen years from 1911–26. Domestic honours included four Scottish Cup medals, six League medals and eleven Charity Cup medals. He played twelve times for Ireland at a time when few international games were played. Both his sons also played football in Scotland – Tommy for Queen's Park and Dundee and Willie for Celtic. He was also the grandfather of Scotland international footballer Kevin Gallacher.

Even more than fifty years after his death, Patsy's name is revered like few others by Celtic fans, most of who were not even born when he died. The term legend seems to underestimate the impact the 'Mighty Atom' had on Celtic and the Celtic faithful.

A plaque commemorating the life and contribution of Patsy Gallacher, the 'Mighty Atom', to the Celtic cause was unveiled on the side of the house in which he grew up in Ramelton, County Donegal.

The unveiling took place on the morning of Monday, 4 June 2007 by a group of the Lisbon Lions and Celtic Chairman Brian Quinn, together with local Ramelton Celtic supporters. There are also plans to erect a statue of Patsy in the centre of the village.

Various writers have compiled many fine accounts of his life and times at the club. The best and the most detailed is called *The Mighty Atom* by David W. Potter.

To play alongside Patsy Gallacher in a national cup final was a dream. Patsy was the fastest man over 10 yards. He moved at great speed and he could stop immediately sending opponents in all directions. He could win a game when the rest of us were just thinking about it.

Jimmy McGrory

He was the greatest who ever kicked a ball.

Tommy Cairns of Rangers

Mickey Hamill

Mickey Hamill was born in Leeson Street, just off the Falls Road in west Belfast. Described, as an outstanding defender, he was one of the most instinctive footballers ever to grace the green and white. He could do what he liked with the ball: clever trapping; accurate passing; back-heeling and wonderful head work. He signed for Belfast Celtic in 1908. Celtic expressed an interest in him in 1910 but he had already pledged himself to Manchester United. He won his first of five Irish caps against England in 1912. Hamill returned to Belfast Celtic on loan in 1913 before joining Celtic on loan on 19 October 1916. He went back to Manchester on 2 December 1916 before returning north again to Celtic on 9 December 1916. Hamill once again returned to Belfast to join Distillery at the end of 1916. He made his last appearances for Celtic on 18 and 25 May 1918 when he was yet again loaned out. From his time in Glasgow Hamill took away with him a Charity Cup medal won on 25 May 1918 to go with his 1916 Championship medal as mementos of his time with Celtic. Celtic fans adored his style of play but sadly Hamill only ever made seven appearances for the club. He retired as a player in 1930 while with Belfast Celtic and became manager of Distillery in 1934. While living at 116 Falls Road, Belfast, the body of Mickey Hamill was discovered drowned in the Lagan Canal at Lurgan. The mystery surrounding his death remains unsolved.

Francis J. Collins
Francis Collins hailed from Dublin. He played in goal for the local Dublin clubs of Wanderers and Jacobs. Collins came to the attention of Celtic while keeping a clean sheet for Junior Ireland against Scotland at Parkhead on 12 March 1921. He was signed as cover for Charlie Shaw on 2 May 1921. He made his Celtic debut on 6 September 1921 in the 4–0 win over Dumbarton. His only other senior appearance came on 19 November in a 3–1 victory over Queens Park. As a Celtic reserve Collins was capped for Ireland at senior level against

Scotland at Parkhead on 4 March 1922 but was put up for transfer at the end of the season. It was said 'Charlie Shaw's too good to give that Dublin lad a look in'. Collins returned to Dublin in 1922 to play again for Jacobs where he won five Free State caps. He was still playing for Jacobs when he retired in 1932.

Peter Kavanagh

Peter Kavanagh was born in Dublin. He was recruited for Bohemians by ex-Ranger Bobby Parker in 1927. Kavanagh was the youngest member of the Bohs' 'Clean Sweep' team of 1927/28 and played against Celtic in a friendly at Dalymount Park on 28 April 1928. Alec Maley was sent to Ireland to watch a fullback in 1929 and reported home on the wonder kid seen at outside left. James Kelly and Tom Colgan crossed over to Ireland to have a look and made the signing, even though wee Peter didn't want to leave his native Dublin. Kavanagh's Celtic debut came on 10 August 1929 against Hearts in a 2–1 league victory. Peter scored his first goal for Celtic against Aberdeen at Parkhead on 24 August 1929 with a bullet 'that almost tore the roof off the net'. He took over from Willie Hughes in the quest for a replacement for Adam McLean but did not develop into what was expected.

Peter was capped twice for Ireland in 1931, each time versus Spain (in Barcelona on 26 April and Dublin on 11 December). He made thirty-five senior appearances for Celtic, scoring ten goals. He left Celtic in May 1932 and continued playing with Northampton Town, 1932, Guildford City, 1933, Hibernian, 1934, Stranraer, 1935 and Waterford City, 1936.

PLAYERS AND STAFF FROM IRELAND AND OF IRISH DESCENT

Willie Cook

Willie Cook was born in Coleraine, Co.Derry. As a right full-back, with the ball control of any inside forward, he was a master at play. He joined Port Glasgow Juniors in 1928 but with Celtic having a chronic problem filling Willie McStay's boots at right back, the Derry man joined Celtic on 13 February 1930. Cook made his league debut in the 4–0 home win over Ayr United on 18 February 1930. His first full season was in the 1931 cup-winning team, which was fondly regarded by Jimmy McGrory as 'the best side he had ever played with'. Willie Cook played in the Celtic team on the day of Johnny Thomson's fatal accident at Ibrox and was called up to the Northern Ireland team in September 1932. On 30 December 1932 he joined Everton. His departure was a total shock. No one could recall when Celtic had ever sold one of its best players mid-season. Cook won an FA Cup medal on 24 April 1933 and played against Celtic in the Exhibition Trophy final at Ibrox on 10 June 1938. In all, Willie Cook had played 110 times for Celtic in his short Scottish career. He ended his football with Southport in 1945. As a coach in the 1950s Cook was in charge of the national teams of Peru and Iraq.

James Foley

James Foley came from Cork. He began his football in Ireland playing for both Belfast Celtic and his native Cork City. In May 1934 he was signed by Celtic. He played in goal and had just won the FAI Cup with Cork before his move to Glasgow. He mostly featured in the reserve team set up at Celtic Park, but he was more than a competent goalkeeper.

He was a fine understudy to Joe Kennaway and a popular figure among his team-mates. An Irish international, he made his competitive Celtic debut in a 4–0 league victory over Airdrie at Celtic Park on 19 October 1935. He departed Celtic in December 1936 for Plymouth after only six appearances for Celtic. He would return to Ireland where he enjoyed much success with Cork.

John Doherty

John Doherty was born in Derry. As an amateur at Derry City, John 'Pot' Doherty was understudy to ex-Celtic goalie Jock Wallace and took over from Tom Doyle in the Celtic reserves. He got his chance after Kennaway had taken a knocking-about in the Ne'erday game at Ibrox in 1939. His debut came on the 3 January 1939 at Celtic Park. It was Queen's Park's first win over Celtic in twelve years. Doherty's second and last appearance was on the occasion of a Joe Carruth hat-trick versus Partick Thistle in a 3–1 win at Parkhead. He returned to Ireland to play for Coleraine in July 1939.

Hugh Doherty

Born in Buncrana Co. Donegal, Hugh 'Dickie' Doherty was spotted playing with Dundalk by Tommy Brogan and gave Celtic his signature as an amateur on 23 August 1946. He displaced Bobby Evans at outside right, sustained a cut temple on his debut but played with the blood pouring down his face. The wound needed five stitches and Hugh turned out against Queen's Park the following Saturday in a scrumcap.

His debut game involved a 2–0 league home win over Queen of the South on the 4 January 1947. Hugh played for Celtic (Division A) in the Scottish Cup at Dens Park versus Dundee (Division B) on 25 January 1947. Despite the attempts of Celtic to get him to sign, Hugh remained obdurate for better terms and went home to Buncrana in May 1947. With Blackpool, he consented to turn professional but his prospects as a right winger were small; prior to Hugh in May 1947, the Seasiders had signed another outside right – the immortal Stanley Matthews. Injuries forced his retirement while with Raith Rovers in late 1949. In total Hugh made only four appearances for Celtic.

Bernard Cannon

Bernard Cannon came from Buncranna, Co. Donegal. His initial years in football were spent with Buncranna Amateurs, Mile End Athletic and Blantyre Celtic. He was taken on trial by Celtic to play against Birmingham on 1 March 1947. After the death of Celtic Chairman, Tom White, he signed terms on 5 March 1947. Cannon made his debut against Hibernian at Easter Road on 12 April 1947 in a 2–0 defeat. His only other appearances for Celtic were against Falkirk on 26 April and Motherwell on 13 May of the same year. Outside lefts were in plentiful supply at Parkhead and Cannon was considered surplus to requirements. He was given a free transfer and returned to Ireland to play for Derry City in May 1948. He played in the Irish Cup Final of 1949 against a Glentoran team that included the great Bertie Peacock. Cannon's final appearance on the turf of Celtic Park came on 24 April 1950 when

Derry City played a friendly against Celtic. He ended his career with Alloa in 1950.

Charlie Tully

Charlie Tully was born in Belfast on 11 July 1924. He played for Belfast Celtic before signing for Celtic on 28 June 1948 for a fee of £8,000. He was idolised by a Celtic support that had been starved of success in the seasons before the Irishman's arrival. He was a remarkable entertainer with a deft repertoire of audacious tricks and feints.

Charlie made his debut on 11 August 1948 in a 0–0 league fixture against Morton at Parkhead. His first goal came on 4 September in a 3–3 draw with Albion Rovers. The skill of Charlie Tully earned him the reputation of a Celtic great in a 3–1 victory over Rangers in the League Cup tie of 25 September 1948 and their so-called 'iron curtain defence'.

It was reported, 'Tully dribbled at will . . . the miraculous Irishman bewildered, badgered and mesmerised Rangers'. This game catapulted Tully to the status of a cult hero and so began 'Tully Mania'. Tully cocktails were sold in Celtic pubs, Tully ties sold in drapery shops and green and white Tully ice cream in cafes.

He took all the corners for Celtic and would more often than not place the ball as far outside the 'D' as possible, if officials didn't notice. One such occasion was against Falkirk in a Scottish Cup tie on 2 February 1953. With Celtic losing 2–0 he took an in-swinging corner that went straight into the net. The referee, spotting an infringement, ordered him to take it again. He did and repeated the remarkable feat. This time the goal stood. Jimmy McGrory and Willie Fernie went on to win the game for Celtic 3–2. Incidentally, the following season while playing for Northern Ireland against England in Belfast with the same referee in charge, Charlie scored direct from a corner again.

The match report read:

> Tully took a corner with his right foot. The in-swinger sailed waist high and at speed, swerving into goal at the last moment. Merrick sensed the danger . . . but the swerving ball bounced out of his arms and over the line.

He was part of the great 'Hampden in the sun' team that thumped Rangers 7–1 in the League Cup final of 9 October 1957 alongside Sean Fallon and Bertie Peacock. Charlie Tully's last goal for his beloved Celtic came on 16 August 1958 against St Mirren. His last appearance was on 31 January 1959 in a first round Scottish Cup tie against Albion Rovers, which Celtic won 4–0. Tully spent brief spells on loan before being freed in September 1959. He moved back to Ireland to manage Cork Hibs before spells with Bangor and Portadown. The great man had played 319 times for Celtic, scoring forty-three goals. He was also capped ten times for Northern Ireland.

Charlie Tully died in his sleep at home in Belfast on 27 July 1971. John Rafferty, writing in *The Observer* remarked, 'it was strange he should have gone out so peacefully. It was not his way of life.' The Falls Road was packed with mourners for his funeral. Johnny Bonnar turned to Jock Stein and said, 'Charlie would have loved this Jock'.

Bertie Peacock

Robert 'Bertie' Peacock was born in Coleraine, Co. Derry in 1928 and arrived at Celtic Park in May of 1949 from Coleraine. He made his Celtic debut at Celtic Park in a 3–1 League Cup defeat against Aberdeen in August 1949. Initially Peacock played as an inside left and formed an effective partnership with Charlie Tully. However he was switched to left half for the 1953/54 season and it was in this position that Peacock revelled.

Nicknamed 'the little ant' due to his amazing work rate, he was an inspirational force within the Celtic team. His excellent close control, good dribbling skills and cool head allowed Peacock to dictate the play from deep and his fitness and stamina were second to none. In his first two years at Celtic Peacock played his part in giving the team its first major success since before World War II when Celtic beat Motherwell 1–0 in the Scottish Cup final of 1951. He played at inside left in the team that won the Coronation Cup in 1953. Peacock won the League Cup in 1956, then, after the sacking of Evans as club captain, was appointed to the job mid-Atlantic en route to the U.S.A on board the S.S. Mauretania.

Peacock remained as Celtic captain until 1961, when he left the club to return to Coleraine. Bertie was a Protestant, but was by no means the first Protestant to captain Celtic, though he was the first from Northern Ireland to do so. He was part of the great Celtic 'Hampden in the Sun' team of 1957 that trounced Rangers 7–1 in the League Cup final. In October 2001 Celtic organised a reunion for the remaining members of that famous team. Four of these greats – Peacock, Fallon,

Collins and Fernie – walked onto the turf of Celtic Park to a heroes' welcome.

Peacock scored fifty goals in his 453 appearances for Celtic. He played thirty-two times for Northern Ireland. He went on to manage Northern Ireland from 1962 until 1967, giving George Best his first international cap. Peacock returned to Coleraine as manager for twelve years, winning them the Irish League title in 1974 before retiring from the game. He was instrumental in starting the Milk Cup tournament in Northern Ireland which has developed into one of youth football's most prestigious competitions. Peacock then managed a pub, but sold it on in 1990 to concentrate on golf. Bertie Peacock died on 22 July 2004 aged seventy-five of a heart attack after a hip operation.

The bronze statue of Bertie Peacock was unveiled in his home town of Coleraine by his son Russell and Pat Jennings. The plinth at the bottom is inscribed 'Sportsman, Statesman, Gentleman'.

Sean Fallon

Sean Fallon was born in Sligo Town on 31 July 1922. His father John was an active local councillor and a former mayor of Sligo Town. In his early years Sean played local soccer with St Mary's juniors and Gaelic football with Craobh Ruadh before joining his native Sligo Town from Longford Town as an amateur in 1949. In the same year he signed professional terms with Glenavon in the Irish League. On 17 March 1950 he was selected to represent an Irish League selection against a League of Ireland selection. After that game, at the age of twenty-eight, Sean Fallon joined Glasgow Celtic, where he would play until 1958 when, at the age of thirty-six, he was forced to retire due to injury.

Sean said of his signing with Celtic, 'I can never hope to find words to express my feelings at becoming a member of the Celtic Football Club,' a statement that still holds Sean in high esteem with Celtic fans to this day.

Sean's arrival at Celtic was indeed a remarkable story and one in which fate would play a part. Joe McMenemy, son of Celtic legend 'Napoleon' (Jimmy McMenemy) was in Sligo when he rescued Lilly Fallon from drowning in Lough Gill. The grateful Fallons invited Joe to their home where he first met Sean. They inevitably must have chatted about the story of fellow Sligo man Brother Walfrid and his legacy of Celtic Football Club. When Joe returned to Scotland he sent a club jersey and Willie Maley's book over to Sean as presents.

When Celtic came calling in 1950, Sean was offered £10 a week, which fell to £8 a week in the close season; he was also offered £1 a week towards his digs. Yet, in Sligo, he earned £8 a week as a confectioner (his trade) and £6 a week playing with Glenavon. But to sign for Celtic meant that he would realise his boyhood dream, so he readily accepted Jimmy McGrory's offer.

Sean made his debut on 15 April 1950 against Clyde in the fullback position and promptly scored an own goal. He would alter this position for a role up front from time to time. Throughout his playing career he was known as the 'Iron Man' – no rolling around the park, no feigning injury, no unfair career-threatening challenges but simply a belief in the jersey and a will to do well for Celtic.

His playing career was ended in 1958 after a serious knee injury and three operations, but he would become the assistant manager to Jock Stein in 1965. Fallon was an integral part of Celtic's success under Jock Stein, when he was the manager's right-hand man and his powers of persuasion were often called upon to secure the signatures of promising young players who would go on to become Celtic legends – David Hay, Danny McGrain, Kenny Dalglish, and Packie Bonner among others. When Jock Stein survived a near-fatal car crash in 1975, Fallon took over as caretaker manager before taking up an appointment with Dumbarton Football Club.

Sean Fallon had made 242 appearances for Celtic, winning two Scottish Cup medals, two League Cup medals, a Scottish League medal and a St Mungo Cup medal. He was also capped for Ireland eight times. But he is most definitely remembered, in his retiring years, as both a Sligo man and a most loyal Celt.

He once assessed his own talents as a player by saying:

I was just an ordinary player with a big heart and a fighting spirit to recommend me.

Sean Fallon recalls his memories of the 7–1 League Cup win over Rangers in 1957.

I remember that game as if it was yesterday. It was the best performance in my time as a Celtic player. Maybe it was because a lot of us were getting old and we realised we didn't have very long to make a real impact.

We never expected to win by such a margin but as the game progressed the confidence grew sky-high. Everything clicked and it seemed we couldn't do anything wrong. It was unbelievable. We were in the doldrums, yet we never went into an Old Firm game believing we were second-best.

Charlie Tully used to get a hard time from Rangers skipper Bobby Shearer. When it was over Bobby said to me 'you moved him because he was afraid of me' but I said we moved him because we wanted to win the game. It was a winning switch because Bobby used to give Charlie little room to operate in.

Bobby was a good defender and a hard man, and so was I, but I don't suppose we would get away with our tackles nowadays although we both played within the laws of the game!

On John Valentine he commented: It destroyed him but I thought it was a shame he took all the blame.

In 2008 Sean Fallon accepted the position of Honorary President of the Association of Irish Celtic Supporters Clubs.

Eamon McMahon

Eamon McMahon was born in Lurgan, Co. Armagh. He played Gaelic football as a goalkeeper for Clan na Gael in Lurgan and for his home county, Armagh. He played for Armagh in the All-Ireland Football final on 27 September 1953 against Kerry at Croke Park, Dublin. Although Armagh lost 0–13 to 1–6, Eamon went into the *Guinness Book of Records* as the one and only 'keeper to play in every round of the All-Ireland tournament without conceding a goal'.

As the son of ex-Glenavon goalkeeper, Peter McMahon, his pedigree was exceptional and his display at Croke Park convinced Celtic's Irish scout Peter O'Connor that Eamon

McMahon was destined for Parkhead. He was signed by Celtic on 30 December 1953 for a signing-on fee of £2,000 and a weekly wage of £12. He played his first game at Parkhead with the reserves on 17 October 1953 against Raith Rovers reserves. Eamon got his first team chance when Johnny Bonnar injured his arm in training. He made his one and only appearance for Celtic on 16 October 1954 against Queen of the South at Parkhead. As a goalkeeper, he had a nightmare: 'I advanced from goal as Black shot from the edge of the penalty box. I had the ball covered low down to my right. As I dived I got both hands to it but to my horror, the ball squirmed from my grasp and wriggled over the line.' He was given a free transfer on 14 May 1955.

While at Celtic, Eamon met his future wife, Patricia Dowdell, the daughter of Celtic trainer Alex Dowdell. He was signed by Glentoran on 4 June 1955, where he had a better time. He lived in Leicester and travelled to Belfast at the weekends to play for Glentoran. Nuneaton Borough wanted him but Glentoran were reluctant to let him go. He retired from football and joined his father in business in Lurgan in 1960 and today is a greyhound trainer.

Joseph Haverty

Joseph 'Joe' Haverty was born in Dublin on 17 February 1936. His start in football was with Dublin club Home Farm in 1951 from where he went to Saint Patrick's Athletic, also Dublin in 1953. Haverty was signed by Arsenal in 1954 where he stayed until 1961 making 236 appearances scoring fifty-one goals. Between 1961 and 1964 he played for Blackburn Rovers and Millwall. At this time Celtic had two left wingers of unfulfilled potential in Bobby Lennox and John Hughes. The club took the decision to take Joe to Parkhead on a month's trial in September 1964 in an attempt to solve this problem. His only game for Celtic came on 17 October 1964 in a 4–1 home victory against St Mirren. Celtic fans were hugely impressed by his one try-out but what happened next is unclear: did Millwall order him home from the Jungle to the Den? Was Celtic repelled by a transfer fee of £3,000? Whichever way, Parkhead cancelled his resignation on 31 October 1964.

When at Parkhead, Dubliner Joe was capped by the Republic of Ireland against Poland on 25 October 1964 and appears in some international record books as Haverty (Glasgow Celtic). Nonetheless, Joe finished up at Celtic and moved to Bristol Rovers, Shelbourne and Chicago Spurs before going to Kansas City Spurs in 1968. He returned to Ireland to sign for Shamrock Rovers in 1969, where he made two appearances in the UEFA Cup Winners' Cup.

In 2000 he was inaugurated into the Football Association of Ireland's Hall of Fame. He died on 7 February 2009, in London, aged seventy-two.

John Kennedy

John Kennedy came from Newtownards, Co Antrim. A goalkeeper, he first played with Distillery in Belfast and took part in the 1964 Tokyo Olympics for the Great Britain Team. When Jock Stein took over as manager of Celtic, Kennedy was signed from Distillery for a fee of £5,000 in March 1965. With John Fallon well established as Celtic's first choice goalkeeper, the

Newtownards man got little chance to impress. His only first team appearance was on 22 September 1965 in the 4–0 home win over Raith Rovers. John Colram of the Detroit Cougars took him on loan for a US soccer tournament and soon after, on 14 July 1967, Kennedy signed for Lincoln City where he played 251 times. He retired on 1 May 1984 after seventeen years in the game without a booking or caution.

Packie Bonner

Patrick Joseph Bonner was born in Clochgas Co. Donegal on 24 May 1960. Until the arrival of Artur Boruc, Packie Bonner was unarguably regarded as the best Celtic goalkeeper since the great Ronnie Simpson. Coming from Donegal, which has had strong links with emigration to Glasgow and a big Celtic support within the county, it's not surprising that Packie Bonner should make such a huge impact in the east end of Glasgow.

Bonner joined Celtic in 1978 from his local side Keadue Rovers and, somewhat appropriately, made his debut on St Patrick's Day 1979 in a 2–1 win at home against Motherwell. A former goalkeeper for the Republic of Ireland, who earned eighty caps after making his debut on his twenty-first birthday, many remember Bonner for his famous penalty save from Daniel Timofte of Romania in the 1990 World Cup finals in Italy.

At club level, Bonner played for Keadue Rovers in his native Donegal, Leicester City, Celtic, and Kilmarnock. He went on to play 642 times for Celtic. With Celtic, he won four League Championship medals, three Scottish Cup winner's medals and a League Cup winner's medal. His last appearance for

Celtic was winning the 1995 Scottish Cup final under Tommy Burns against Airdrie.

On 2 February 2003, Packie was named as the Technical Director and Goalkeeping Coach for the Football Association of Ireland. In addition, he has more recently made a career as a football presenter with TV3 Ireland.

Pierce O'Leary

Pierce O'Leary was born in Dublin. He was signed by Davie Hay from Vancouver Whitecaps in 1984. He made his Celtic debut on 30 January 1985. O'Leary featured skilfully beside Roy Aitken in the Celtic defence, when he came on as a substitute in the Scottish Cup Final of 1985, when Celtic beat Dundee United 2–1. He won a Scottish Cup winner's medal in 1985 and was part of the League Championship winning side of 1986.

The next season pelvic problems limited O'Leary's chances for selection, but he still made enough appearances to claim a League Championship medal after Celtic pipped Hearts for the title on the final day. When Billy McNeill returned as Celtic manager in the summer of 1987, O'Leary had already slipped from the first team picture and, as injuries continued to plague the player, his time at Celtic was coming to a close. He was released by Celtic in May 1988 after making forty-nine appearances and scoring one goal. He would retire later that year having never found another club after Celtic. He is the brother of David O'Leary, who was capped seven times for Ireland between 1979 and 1980.

Allen McKnight

Allen McKnight was born in Belfast on 27 January 1964. He kept goal for Distillery in Belfast for two seasons, making sixty-eight appearances. He signed for Celtic in August 1986. McKnight found himself as third choice goalkeeper behind Pat Bonner and Peter Latchford. He was loaned out for the season to Albion Rovers. His time in the Scottish Second Division earned McKnight valuable experience in the Scottish game and a Lanarkshire Cup winner's medal.

He got his opportunity at Parkhead when Packie Bonner went down with a virus in August 1987. McKnight made his debut against Dumbarton in a 5–1 away League Cup game on 26 August 1987. Three days later he made his Premier Division debut, keeping a clean sheet in the heat of an Old Firm derby, Celtic beating Rangers 1–0. Ultimately, Packie Bonner recovered and reclaimed his place as first choice goalkeeper, but McKnight's twelve appearances and five clean sheets helped the Championship trophy return to Parkhead.

1987/88 also saw Allen McKnight make his international debut for Northern Ireland, displacing George Dunlop for the European Championship qualification match with Yugoslavia in October 1987. He played every minute of that season's internationals, six in all, and kept clean sheets against Turkey, France and Malta. The highlight of McKnight's season was to come in the Scottish Cup final. Packie Bonner had picked up calf and hamstring injuries in training just days before the Scottish Cup final. Billy McNeill kept the injury a secret right up to the day of the final. Allen McKnight made a surprise appearance between the posts. Celtic claimed the trophy, and the double, with a 2–1 victory over Dundee United.

In July 1988, with Packie Bonner still Celtic's obvious goal-keeping choice, McKnight jumped at the chance to play top flight football in England, with West Ham United manger John Lyall paying £250,000 for his services.

McKnight made seventeen appearances for Celtic when his career then took him around many clubs before finishing with Exeter City in 1994. When Allen played for Northern Ireland at Windsor Park he was subject to taunts of 'traitor', a reference to him being a Protestant and playing for Celtic.

Anton Rogan

Anton Rogan was born in the Lenadoon Area of West Belfast on 25 March 1966. His football career began with Distillery in Belfast. He played his international football with Northern Ireland. A journalist once described the reception given to him as the worst ever given to an international player anywhere at any time. Anton's only crime was to be a Roman Catholic playing for Celtic.

Signed by Celtic in 1986, Anton Rogan made 148 appearances in the hoops, making his debut in the trophy-less season of 1986/87 under the then boss Davie Hay. He was originally expected to sign for Celtic in 1994, but with successive leg breaks with Distillery, the move was put on hold. He established himself as a first-team regular when Billy McNeill replaced Hay as Celtic manager in the summer of 1987.

Rogan quickly impressed the new manager and established himself as a first-team regular. Though three of his five seasons at Parkhead were barren, Rogan collected three winners' medals and enjoyed a fair degree of success at the expense of Rangers, whose fans are still inclined to sneer at the mention of his name. Few moments in his career were sweeter than when he opened the scoring against 'them' in a league encounter back in March 1991. Billy McNeill's side had galvanised themselves after a poor first half to the season and kept their hope of silverware alive by dismissing Graeme Souness's Rangers 2–0 in a Scottish Cup quarter-final tie in which four players were red-carded.

When the sides met for a second successive Sunday at Celtic Park on league business, Rangers were looking for revenge but Rogan's early strike put them on the back foot and goals from Joe Miller and Tommy Coyne wrapped up another emphatic win.

Rogan remembers: 'It wasn't the most stylish goal you ever saw, Tommy Coyne got a touch from a corner and the ball dropped to me. I hooked it towards goal and it trickled past Chris Woods. But the feeling couldn't have been any better if I'd rattled it in from thirty yards. I just went daft.'

Another game Rogan recalls with affection is a 2–1 win at Ibrox, which went a long way towards sealing the Centenary Season title in 1987/88. With the score level 1–1 and little over ten minutes remaining, he soared above the Rangers defence to meet a corner kick. Anton being Anton, he didn't simply power it into the net, but glanced it down to Andy Walker who redirected the ball into the net with his chest in true poacher's fashion. 'I was aiming for the badge in Andy's shirt!' says Rogan, tongue firmly in cheek.

Celtic never built on that double success though, and, like many of his teammates, Rogan would spend the next few seasons as part of a Celtic team which struggled to keep up with a Rangers team supported by a level of finance and ambition which the Parkhead board had no intention of matching. Rogan's form and confidence suffered as the mediocre Celtic quickly became sorry also-rans in the quest for domestic honours. Rogan, now no longer a first-team regular under new boss Liam Brady, eventually left Glasgow in 1991 to join Sunderland in a £750,000 deal.

Anton Rogan had spent five years with Celtic, two years with Sunderland, two years with Oxford, two years with Millwall and a final two with Blackpool.

It was a career that I dreamt of as a schoolboy. I was part of the Celtic side that won the double in 1988 during the club's centenary year. That is very special to me. I have no regrets from my career. I've played in a Scottish Cup final, which we won, and an FA Cup final, which Sunderland unfortunately lost; very few players achieve that during their career. My disappointment of course would be that penalty miss against Aberdeen in the Scottish Cup Final which everybody seems to remember when my spot kick lost the cup to Aberdeen.

Liam Brady

Liam 'Chippy' Brady was born in Dublin on 13 February 1956. He came from a football family with both his great uncle Frank Brady and older brother Ray Brady having been Irish internationals. His older brother Frank won the FAI Cup with Shamrock Rovers in 1968 and made two appearances in the UEFA Cup Winners' Cup, while another brother, Pat Brady, played with QPR. Young Liam grew up in the north of Dublin, just a few hundred yards from two other Irish lads, David O'Leary and Frank Stapleton, who would both later become his teammates at Arsenal.

Liam Brady started his football career with St Kevin's Boy's and Home Farm in his native Dublin. His talent was spotted at the tender age of thirteen, whilst playing for St Kevin's Boys Club Under-Fifteens. Arsenal scout Bill Darby is reputed to have claimed Brady 'has a left foot that practically talks.'

Brady began his career in England, with Arsenal, joining the club on schoolboy forms at the age of fifteen in 1970. He signed as a professional on his seventeenth birthday in 1973. He made his Arsenal debut aged seventeen, on 6 October 1973 against Birmingham City. By 1974 Liam was a regular first team player. Renowned for his elegant technical skills, most notably his famous left foot, his quality passing and close control, he gained the nickname 'Chippy', although this was on account of this dietary habits rather than his ability to chip the ball.

With the Gunners, Brady won the 1979 FA Cup, as well as being runner up in the 1978 and 1980 finals. He was also on the losing Arsenal side against Valencia in the Cup Winners' Cup final of 1980. Arsenal lost on a penalty shoot out with Brady missing a spot kick. He was a talented player with an average Arsenal side, which failed to challenge for any serious honours. He was voted the club's player of the year three times and the PFA Player of the Year in 1979.

In the summer of 1980 Brady signed for Italian giants, Juventus, and spent two seasons there, picking up two Italian Championship medals in 1981 and 1982. After the arrival of Michel Platini in the summer of 1982, Brady moved to Sampdoria, then to Internazionale (1984–1986) and Ascoli

(1986–1987) before returning to London to play for West Ham (1987–1990). He won seventy-two international caps for the Republic of Ireland, scoring nine goals, although he never played in a major tournament, thanks to injury and a suspension before Euro 1988.

After retiring from playing in 1990, he managed Celtic for an unsuccessful term from 1991–1993 and then Brighton & Hove Albion from 1993–1995. Both tenures were overshadowed by financial problems at each club, it would seem. Brady is remembered as one of Arsenal's all-time greats but sadly not as a great Celtic manager. Today he works as a television pundit, Arsenal's head of youth development and as assistant to Republic of Ireland manager Giovanni Trapattoni.

Mick Martin

Mick Martin was born in Dublin. He was first team coach of Celtic during the unsuccessful reign of Liam Brady. His career spanned from 1972 until 1985 with spells at Manchester United, West Bromwich Albion, Newcastle, Cardiff, Peterborough, Rotherham, and Preston. He became coach at Newcastle United and then Celtic and now lives in Newcastle where he is a radio show host. He played fifty-two times for Ireland with his first game against Austria in 1971 and his final game against Spain in 1983.

Shay Given

Shay Given was born in Lifford, Co. Donegal on 20 April 1976. He began his youth football in Donegal with Lifford. At the tender age of fifteen, he was invited on a pre-season tour of Ireland with Celtic. The teenager trained with the hoops during the club's pre-season trip to Ireland and decided to join the Parkhead club rather than take up offers from any of a host of top English clubs. Arsenal, Aston Villa and Manchester United were among the sides south of the border keen to sign the Republic of Ireland youth international. But the time spent with Celtic in Dublin and Cork seemed to sway the young Given.

In September 1992 Celtic signed sixteen-year-old goalkeeper Shay Given from Packie Bonner's home county of Donegal.

Liam Brady said: 'I'm a great believer in coincidences. Shay's the best keeper to come out of Ireland since Packie – and they're both from Donegal.'

Shay was highly regarded during his time at Celtic Park and was considered as the natural successor to Pat Bonner. However, then Celtic manager Lou Macari thought Stewart Kerr was the better long term option and allowed Shay Given to leave the club on a free transfer for Blackburn Rovers in 1994. After impressing Kenny Dalglish there, the former Celtic and Liverpool legend moved to management with Newcastle United and accordingly made Shay Given one of his first signings. Shay made 354 appearances for the magpies before signing for Manchester City on 1 February 2009. He made his debut for City on 7 February 2009, keeping a clean sheet against Middlesbrough, earning him the Man of the Match accolade.

Paul Byrne

Paul Byrne was born in Dublin on 3 June 1972. His football career started with the amateur club Bluebell United in his native city. He joined Oxford United in 1986 on a Youth Training Scheme and went on to sign professional terms in 1988. Byrne was at the Manor Ground for five seasons and played under three managers. In 1990 he was offered a free transfer and was signed by Bangor of the Irish League. He excelled there, winning the accolades of the Soccer Writers' Northern Ireland Player of the Year and Young Northern Ireland Player of the Year. Byrne came to the attention of Celtic and signed for £70,000 in the summer of 1993. 'I really couldn't believe it when Celtic came looking for me, and the move to Parkhead was the highlight of my career'.

Byrne made his first start for the hoops on 6 October 1993 against St Johnstone in a 2–1 defeat. Paul scored his first Celtic goal on 19 January 1994 against Aberdeen but is best remembered for his stunning goal against arch rivals Rangers in the 1995 New Year old firm match. The move to Celtic earned him a call up by the Irish manager, Jack Charlton, to join the squad for an international against Russia, although he failed to get any action.

In total Paul Byrne made twenty-four appearances for Celtic. He went to Brighton & Hove Albion on loan and was later transferred to Southend United for a fee of £80,000. He stayed two seasons at Roots Hall before returning to Northern Ireland to join Glenavon. It was then back to the League of Ireland with Bohemians, St Patrick's Athletic, Kilkenny City and finally Dundalk on 11 March 2003.

Ashley Grimes
Ashley Grimes was born in Dublin on 2 August 1957. He was in charge of the Celtic Youth and Under-twenty-one teams in

1994/95. This was during Lou Macari's stint as Celtic manager. He has spent twenty-four years in professional football, with Manchester United, Coventry City, Luton Town, Osasuna in Spain and Stoke City. He earned seventeen international caps with the Republic of Ireland, won an FA Cup medal with Manchester United, a League Cup medal with Luton Town, and an Autoglass Cup medal with Stoke City.

Declan Boyle

Declan Boyle was born in Killybegs, Co. Donegal on 12 February 1974. He had won Republic of Ireland Schoolboy caps and was awarded the Football Association of Ireland Schoolboy of the Year Award in 1992. He joined Sligo Rovers and played a key role in the side that won the FAI Cup, First Division Championship and Shield in 1994. The then Sligo manager, Willie McStay, rated the young defender very highly and, on moving back to Glasgow, recommended that Celtic sign the young Killybegs man.

Boyle joined Celtic in January 1995 for a reported fee of £65,000 and spent three years there. Although he never progressed to the first team, he did win a reserve League Cup medal and was always a stalwart in the reserves defence. At the age of twenty-two Boyle left Celtic and returned to Ireland in 1997 to join Derry City where he remained for six months before returning to Donegal and signing for Finn Harps.

James Gallagher

James Gallagher was born in Lower Meenlarragh just outside the village of Gortahork in north-west Donegal on 13 February

1980. He represented the Republic of Ireland at under fifteen, under sixteen and under eighteen level. His soccer honours in Ireland were an AIB Ulster Senior Cup with Falcarragh Community School and two successive Donegal Youth League Championship medals with Gleanea United Youths in 1994 and 1995.

Michael McGinley, his coach at Falcarragh, alerted Willie McStay, head youth coach with Celtic of James' exceptional talent. James was asked to attend a coaching session in Sligo under the watchful eyes of Willie McStay, David Hay and Peter Latchford, who confirmed his unquestionable ability. He travelled to Glasgow during school breaks for the next eighteen months for coaching by Packie Bonner. James was offered a contract with Celtic and signed apprentice forms in July 1996 in the Abbey Hotel in Donegal Town. Unfortunately, he never progressed to finish his apprenticeship.

Liam Miller

Liam Miller was born in Cork City on 13 February 1981, the same city as Roy Keane, whom he idolised. Miller joined Celtic as a sixteen-year-old youth player in October 1997 and eventually made his league debut in the final game of the 1999/00 season as a substitute against Dundee United. He had to wait until 2003/04 before being elevated to the first team on a full-time basis.

Former Celtic defender Marc Rieper took him on loan to AFG Åarhus in 2001/02, where he made eighteen appearances during his spell with the Danish club. On his return to Scotland, the Irishman was a revelation, especially in the

Champions League where he produced a number of 'man of the match' performances. He scored on his Champions League debut against FBK Kaunas in the 2003/04 second qualifying round, and played all four qualifying matches as Celtic claimed a place in the group stages of the competition. He then started the season in the first team and scored again against Olympique Lyonnais.

In January 2004 Miller signed a pre-contract agreement with Manchester United. An official announcement came after Sir Alex Ferguson persuaded the twenty-two-year-old to join the Premiership champions rather than agreeing a new contract with Celtic. Miller was injury prone, which held back his career, and when the crunch time came for contract negotiations, a variety of events and issues happened which led to his decision to move to Manchester United, the club he supported as a boy. Manchester United was willing to pay him more for a longer contract, which Celtic was not prepared to match. His decision to leave Celtic caused a furore amongst Celtic fans about loyalty and a note of disdain still exists when his name is mentioned.

A slight, but strong-running midfield player, Liam Miller was blessed with good pace and a high level of stamina. Dubbed the new Roy Keane because of his work rate, strength in the tackle and goal-scoring record, the twenty-two-year-old Miller joined Manchester United in July 2004. On releasing Miller on 31 August 2006, Sir Alex Ferguson is quoted as saying 'Liam Miller is no Roy Keane'.

Liam Miller leaving was a devastating blow for everybody. He was such a talented lad and him being allowed to leave was very disappointing for people who are working down below. You get some talent and all of a sudden it's away, à la Maloney, which was the same thing.

Tommy Burns April 2006

Jim Goodwin

Jim Goodwin came from Tramore in Co. Waterford. He was signed by Celtic in 1997.

The centre half made his first senior appearance at the end of season 1999/00 aged eighteen in Celtic's 2–0 league victory over Dundee United at Celtic Park on 21 May, in front of 47,500 fans. While Celtic hadn't enjoyed the best of seasons, Jim's performances for the club's Youth and Reserve sides had seen him deservedly progress through the ranks.

Acting Manager, Kenny Dalglish, gave a literal look to the Bhoys' last line-up of that current campaign by giving Jim and two other youngsters their debuts, and three more their first ever starts (before they had been used as substitutes). Celtic's Director of Football – who made his own professional debut at Parkhead at the age of nineteen – said the new additions to the starting eleven had every reason to be pleased with their performances: 'There are a lot of happy memories there for six young kids.'

Speaking after his first seventy-six minutes as a senior Celt, a delighted Jim said it was 'a day I'll never forget. Playing at Parkhead in front of 47,000 is something that I've been working towards for the last three years. My Dad had travelled over for the game and I was conscious that I wanted to do my best for him, as well as for everyone in Tramore and Waterford.'

In 2002, Jim was the captain of the Under-twenty-one side, which won the League and also captain of the Ireland Under-twenty-one team. After failing to gain first team recognition under Martin O'Neill, he left Parkhead in the summer of 2002 to join Stockport County.

Colin Healy

Colin Healy was born in Ballincollig, Co. Cork on 14 March 1980. He played all his schoolboy football with Ballincollig and represented Cork Schoolboys teams at Under-Thirteen and Under-Fourteen levels. He also played on the Munster Under-Seventeen team. Colin was recommended to the FAS Soccer School where he was spotted by Celtic coach Mick Conroy. He was offered trials with Celtic, which resulted in him been offered a two-year contract. He signed for Celtic on 7 July 1998.

He played for the Irish Youth Team and scored the winning goal against Russia, which sent Ireland through to the European Championships finals in Sweden where they finished third. Colin won eight caps at youth level and then went on to win six caps at Under-Twenty level in the World Championships in Malaysia.

During his two-year stay with Celtic, Colin progressed from the youth team through to the reserves and finally on to the first team when he came on against Rangers at Celtic Park to make his debut. He made his full home debut against Aberdeen at which a large party of Ballincollig supporters were there to see him.

He was beginning to establish himself in the Celtic midfield with some fine performances under interim manager Kenny Dalglish, including a rather glorious goal against Dundee at Dens Park, but disaster struck when Colin damaged knee ligaments in a clash at McDiarmud Park on 13 May. Colin came back and played his part in the treble-winning season of 2000/01, playing in the League Cup final against Kilmarnock. He made his full Irish International against Russia in a friendly in the month of February 2002.

Colin was unable to break into the Celtic team on a regular basis, despite being a regular for Ireland, and left to join Mick McCarthy's Sunderland in August 2003, after making forty-nine appearances for Celtic, scoring one goal. His time at Sunderland also saw the beginning of a cruel series of injuries, the first of which was a broken leg as a result of a horrific challenge by Youssouf Safri in December 2003.

Having recovered from that injury, Healy broke down in training as a result of another broken leg. He managed to recover from his injury hell and joined Livingston in 2005, having gone back home to Cork to consider his future in football. Little more than a year later, he returned home to play for Cork City. Healy was controversially banned from playing for Cork until July 2007 by FIFA under its three-club rule. Cork City appealed, citing the example of Javier Mascherano, who had been available for selection for Liverpool despite having been registered at three different clubs between July and June. FIFA had adjudicated that, as Corinthians played in the January-December league, that he was exempt from that law but bizarrely decided that Healy was not, despite the Eircom League also running from January to December.

Martin O'Neill

Martin O'Neill was born in Kilrea, near Colraine in Co. Derry on 1 March 1952. He played Gaelic football as a youth in Kilrea, winning the famous McGrory Cup in 1970 with St Malachy's College, Belfast, before switching to soccer.

He began a degree in law at Queen's University, Belfast while playing for local side Distillery. O'Neill was spotted by a scout for Nottingham Forest, for whom he signed in 1971, opting to end his studies. Martin made slow progress until the legendary Brian Clough arrived at the City ground in 1975 and made the Derry man a key part of his midfield. Forest gained promotion into England's top flight with O'Neill playing an integral role, then won the League and League Cup in 1978, followed by further League Cup success a year later and the first of two European Cup successes. Sadly, in mitigating circumstances, Martin didn't feature.

O'Neill won sixty-two caps for Northern Ireland, the most notable being as captain in the 1982 World Cup finals in Spain. At club level he also played for Norwich City and Manchester City before retiring. After his playing career, O'Neill entered club management, initially with non-league Wycombe Wanderers, whom he took into the League in 1993. He proceeded to manage Norwich City but resigned on a matter of principle before he could make an impact. O'Neill joined Leicester City in the second half of season 1995/96 where he gained them promotion to the Premiership. Under O'Neill, they also won the League Cup in 1997 and 2000. During his tenure at Leicester, O'Neill famously held talks to become the next Leeds manager, but declined to move. In the summer of 2000 he became the manager of Celtic, taking over the team left by John Barnes and Kenny Dalglish. In his first season he won the treble. In his five seasons at Celtic Park, Celtic won three League titles, culminating in a UEFA Cup final in Seville in 2003.

During his time at Celtic, Martin had been linked continuously with every managerial vacancy in the English Premiership. It was announced on 25 May 2005, that Martin O'Neill would resign as Celtic manager at the end of season 2004/05, following the Scottish Cup final on 28 May against Dundee United. It was time to take a break away from football to care for his wife, Geraldine, who was battling lymphoma. O'Neill's last competitive game in charge of Celtic was the Scottish Cup final 1–0 victory over Dundee United, thanks to an Alan Thompson goal, bringing Martin's tally to seven trophies. And, right on cue, Martin himself lifted the glorious trophy.

Martin O'Neill was awarded an OBE for services to sport in 2004. In August 2006, having been linked with numerous jobs during his time away from the game, including England, he returned to work as manager of Aston Villa and also works as a TV pundit.

Neil Lennon

Neil Francis Lennon was born on 25 June 1971 in Lurgan, Co. Armagh. He progressed through the ranks of professional football, culminating in his present position on the coaching staff of Celtic Football Club. Lennon began his football career with Glenavon in the Irish League in 1989, making two appearances and scoring two goals. He was taken to Manchester by

Manchester City as a trainee later that same year. Lennon made only one appearance for the blue half of the city before joining Crewe Alexandra in 1990, making 147 appearances.

In 1996 Lennon joined Leicester City where fellow Northern Ireland man, Martin O'Neill, was manager. This would prove to be a vital link in the chain when Neil Lennon would later move to Celtic. When Martin O'Neill left Leicester City in the summer of 2000 to take over as manager of Celtic, his first target was Lennon. Despite an eventual £8 million offer to Leicester and generous personal terms to the player, it had seemed that the long-serving midfielder had decided to pledge his future to the Foxes by signing a new long-term deal at Filbert Street. However, the pull of his love for Celtic was too great and he arrived at Celtic Park within a few months of O'Neill.

According to one newspaper, the deal was threatened by a late bid from Chelsea to secure his signature. Leicester's much-publicised 5pm deadline on Tuesday, 5 December alerted Blues boss Claudio Ranieri, who immediately acted on the advice of his boardroom. Despite the lure of a salary alleged to be higher than his reputed £30,000 per week at Leicester, the midfielder would not be swayed from his desire to link up with Martin O'Neill at Celtic.

Lennon won the treble with Celtic in his first season. He became Celtic captain in 2005. On 23 June 2006, Celtic announced he had signed a new one-year contract. Sunderland manager Roy Keane made an attempt to sign Lennon prior to the closure of the August 2006 transfer window, but his approach for the player was rejected by Celtic. On 25 April 2007, Neil Lennon announced he would be leaving Celtic. He ended his service for the club on 26 May 2007 by captaining the team to victory in the Scottish Cup final against Dunfermline Athletic; Celtic's 1–0 win clinched the League and Cup double. He was linked with the vacant manager's job at Hibernian following the resignation of former Celtic great John Collins.

Lennon was capped forty times by Northern Ireland before deciding to retire from international football in August 2002 after receiving a death threat ahead of a Northern Ireland match against Cyprus. Lennon joined Nottingham Forest on a one-year deal with an option for a second year on 12 June 2007. He made his Nottingham Forest debut captaining the side in a 0–0 draw at home to Bournemouth. He missed a week's training with Forest because of family reasons in Scotland and lost his place in the team as a consequence.

Lennon joined Wycombe Wanderers on 31 January 2008 before leaving on 3 April the same year to take up a coaching position at Celtic.

Roy Keane

Roy Maurice Keane was born in Mayfield in Cork City on 10 August 1971.

He first played football for local Cork club Rockmount, before signing for the semi-professional Irish club Cobh Ramblers in 1989. Scouts from Brian Clough's Nottingham Forest took note of his talents and promptly signed him for the sum of £10,000. Keane was quick to impress at Nottingham Forest, making his professional league debut against Liverpool.

In 1991, Keane was a regular in the side, displacing the

English international midfield player Steve Hodge, and scored three goals during a run to that season's FA Cup final, which Forest ultimately lost to Tottenham Hotspur. A year later Keane returned to Wembley with Forest for the League Cup final but again finished on the losing side as Manchester United gained a 1–0 win.

Manchester United and Blackburn Rovers competed to sign Keane after Nottingham Forest's relegation in 1993. Manchester United was successful, signing Keane for a then record £3.75m transfer fee. Keane immediately went into the first team, playing in centre midfield alongside Paul Ince.

After the retirement of Eric Cantona in 1997, Keane became team captain, although he missed most of the 1997–98 season because of a cruciate-ligament injury caused by an attempt to foul the Leeds United player Alf-Inge Haaland.

As Keane lay prone on the ground, Haaland stood over Keane, accusing him of feigning injury. United were top of the league at the time, but their form dropped and they finished the season without a trophy. Keane returned, however, to captain the club to an unprecedented treble in 1999 including the FA Premier League, UEFA Champions League and FA Cup. As recognition for his efforts, Keane was voted PFA Players' Player of the Year in 2000.

In 2001, Keane played against Alf-Inge Haaland for the first time since their clash in 1998 and was sent off for a foul which left Haaland with a serious injury. He subsequently admitted in an autobiography that he intended 'to hurt' Haaland. Although Haaland retired from football shortly afterwards, he had previously stated on his website that the cause of this was a recurring problem in his leg, rather than Keane's tackle. Keane was banned for five matches and fined £150,000.

Although he maintains a low profile off the pitch, Keane was involved in several controversial incidents while at Manchester United. In 1995, he was sent off from an FA Cup semi-final for stamping on Gareth Southgate, for which he was suspended for three matches and fined £5,000. In August 2002 he was fined two weeks wages, £150,000, and suspended for three matches for elbowing Jason McAteer. This caused much anguish in the English press as Keane booked himself in for a hip operation and thus would have missed those three matches anyway.

Keane's trophy haul with Manchester United includes: seven Premiership titles (1994, 1996, 1997, 1999, 2000, 2001, 2003), four FA Cups (1994, 1996, 1999, 2004), a European Cup (1999, though Keane missed the final through suspension) and an Intercontinental Cup (1999). On 5 February 2005, Keane scored his fiftieth goal for Manchester United in a league game against Birmingham City. His appearance in the 2005 FA Cup final (which United lost) was his seventh such game, an all-time record. Keane was also picked on the FIFA 100, a list of the greatest living footballers picked by Pelé.

Most recently, his criticism of several of his fellow Manchester United players after an abject 4–1 defeat at the hands of Middlesbrough was deemed too damning and was subsequently pulled from transmission on United's own TV station, MUTV. Keane is thought to have blasted Rio Ferdinand, John O'Shea, Alan Smith, Kieran Richardson and, perhaps most notably, Darren Fletcher, saying 'I can't see why they all rave about Darren Fletcher in Scotland.' Keane was widely supported by Manchester United fans after the outbursts.

He had announced that he would leave United in the summer of 2006, at the end of his contract with Manchester United. Many people were expecting Keane to fulfil his dream of playing for Celtic when he parted ways with his club of twelve years. He was already training for his UEFA coaching badges. His then manager, Sir Alex Ferguson, had said that he wanted Keane to succeed him as manager when he retires. However, in the wake of Keane's tirade against his own team-mates, Ferguson had gone coy over Keane's prospects as a manager. In November 2005, Ferguson said, 'young managers come along and people say this one will be England manager or boss of this club, but two years later they're not there. It's not an easy environment to come into, I wouldn't forecast anything.'

Keane unexpectedly left Manchester United on 18 November 2005, during a protracted absence from the team due to injury. He played his last game for Manchester United in September 2005, which was a 0–0 draw against rivals Liverpool in which he sustained a broken foot. Keane criticised the club's pre-season trip to Portugal, branding it unprofessional, which triggered an argument with assistant coach and one time Real Madrid manager Carlos Queiroz.

He had already stated his belief that his contract would be the last with the club and the aforementioned MUTV transmission had frosted relations still further. There had also been rumours of Ferguson threatening to strip him of club captaincy for refusing to apologise for his MUTV outburst, although some of the players concerned publicly backed him afterwards.

Manchester United reached an agreement with Roy Keane allowing him to leave the club immediately, and offered him a testimonial in recognition of his twelve and a half years at Old Trafford. The club also thanked him for his major contribution as a player. On 14 December, the BBC reported that Keane would sign with Celtic, after agreeing to sign a contract in the region of £40,000 per week, and he officially became a Celtic player the following day, although the club denied the wage level reported in the media, with Chief Executive Peter Lawwell stating that Keane would 'fit within the current wage structure', which was a maximum wage of £22,500 per week.

At international level, Keane represented his country sixty-six times. He was named Ireland's player of the tournament at the 1994 World Cup in the USA. In 2001, with Roy Keane putting in Man of the Match performances, Ireland went undefeated against international soccer heavyweights Portugal and the Netherlands, famously knocking out the Dutch to qualify for the 2002 World Cup in Japan and Korea.

During the summer of 2002, at a pre-World Cup training camp in Saipan, Keane and Ireland manager Mick McCarthy had a disagreement about the FAI preparations for the World Cup. Keane's dissatisfaction with the Irish preparations first came to light in an interview with *Irish Times* journalist Tom Humphries. Keane later alleged in his autobiography that he felt the Irish fans were 'mocked' by the 'lax attitude' the Irish FA took towards the preparations. After a team meeting at which McCarthy accused Keane of feigning injury, Keane is thought to have responded by insulting McCarthy and questioning his abilities as a manager, although Keane denied this in his autobiography.

McCarthy decided he had no option but to send Keane home, although Keane himself had first quit the squad before being talked around by Manchester United manager Alex Ferguson. Neither during or after the meeting did any other player voice support for Keane, although it's thought that some later conferred their support to him in private. Despite efforts from both the media and prominent Irish politicians, the two protagonists were unable to resolve the matter and Keane missed out on the World Cup and stated that he would not play again for the Republic of Ireland under Mick McCarthy.

The appointment of Brian Kerr as Ireland manager in 2003 eventually led to the controversial return of Keane in the international arena in 2004. He made his international return on 25 May 2004 in a friendly match against Romania at Lansdowne Road. His performances in subsequent matches made him a firm favourite among fans once more. He helped Ireland draw away with France and Switzerland in their 2006 World Cup qualifying campaign.

On 14 October 2005, following Ireland's failure to qualify for the World Cup finals in Germany in 2006, Keane announced his retirement from international football.

Following a highly publicised disagreement with Manchester United boss Sir Alex Ferguson, Roy Keane abruptly parted company with the club on 18 November 2005. He signed for his boyhood favourites Celtic on 15 December 2005 on a free transfer.

'It is a great move for me, I have taken my time but everything is now done – it is a good day,' Keane explained, 'I am looking forward to the challenge.'

In January 2006 Roy Keane would make his debut for his 'beloved' Celtic. That day Celtic crashed to a 2–1 defeat to lowly Clyde in the third round of the Scottish Cup. Keane scored his only Celtic goal a month later in a 2–1 Scottish Premier League victory over Falkirk. He retained his place the following Sunday in his first Old Firm derby, leading Celtic to victory in a typically combative Man of the Match perform-ance. Celtic went on to complete a double of the Scottish Premier League title and Scottish League Cup, his last honour as a player. On 12 June 2006, Roy Keane announced his retire-ment from professional football on medical advice, only six months after joining Celtic. He became manager of Sunderland on 28 August 2006. Following a turbulent spell on the field, Roy decided to step down from management on 4 December 2008, with Sunderland in eighteenth position.

Cillian Sheridan

Cillian Sheridan was born on 23 February 1989 in the town of Bailieborough, Co. Cavan. He played Gaelic football for Bailieboro Shamrocks and was a member of the County Cavan Minor team. He was signed by Celtic on 10 February 2006 from Dublin club Belvedere FC. After scoring freely for the Celtic under-nineteen team, Sheridan was promoted to the reserve team then the first team squad during his first season at the club, a 'spectacular rise' according to Celtic Coach Joe McBride.

Cillian made his first team debut for Celtic in the Scottish Cup against Inverness Caledonian Thistle on 25 February 2007. He signed a new three year contract with the club two days later. He appeared in Celtic's Champions League game against Manchester United on 21 October 2008 at Old Trafford, replacing Scott McDonald in the seventy-seventh minute. On

25 October 2008 Sheridan made his first start for Celtic and marked it with a goal in the thirty-sixth minute in a 4–2 win over Hibernian. On 6 November 2008 he was in the Celtic starting line-up that played Manchester United in the Champions League at Celtic Park. Cillian is currently on loan to Motherwell (at time of writing).

Darren O'Dea

Darren O'Dea was born in Dublin on 4 February 1987. He was signed by Celtic as a trainee from Dublin club Home Farm on 1 August 2005. O'Dea made his Celtic debut in the CIS Cup against St Mirren in September 2006. He made his first league appearance two months later as a substitute against Inverness Caledonian Thistle and made his first league starting appearance against Dunfermline in December 2006, just four days after making his Champions League debut against FC Copenhagen as a substitute, replacing the injured Steven McManus. O'Dea is one of several talented defenders to have emerged from the Celtic Youth Academy. His first goal for Celtic came against Dundee United on 26 December 2006.

Paddy McCourt

Patrick Seamus Kevin Gerald Sean McCourt was born in Derry on 16 December 1983. He is the brother of former Derry City striker Harry McCourt. He was educated at Steelstown Primary School in Derry and began his football career with Foyle Harps before moving to Rochdale on a youth team contract. His potential as a promising winger persuaded the Spotland club to sign him on a three and a half year contract in December 2001.

McCourt was capped nine times at Under-twenty-one level for the Northern Ireland team when in June 2002, the then Northern Ireland manager, Sammy McIlroy, gave him his first senior cap against Spain at Windsor Park. He attracted the attention of several Premier League clubs in 2002/03, including Blackburn Rovers and Manchester City. The offers were rejected by Rochdale. In the 2003/04 seasons, McCourt managed just a handful of starts for the club and had two spells away on trial with English First Division sides Norwich City and Crewe Alexandra, though neither club followed up their initial interest in him. Despite scoring some spectacular goals during his spell at Spotland Stadium, a combination of injuries and loss of form hastened his departure from Rochdale in February 2005.

After Rochdale manager Steve Parkin had informed him that he was to be released, McCourt headed for another trial, this time with Motherwell. Again a move failed to materialise after a two-week stay at Fir Park, but shortly afterwards his career was thrown a lifeline when he was signed by Roddy Collins, manager of Eircom League full-timers Shamrock Rovers. A rejuvenated McCourt wasted no time in becoming a firm favorite with the Rovers fans when he scored three goals in his first six appearances for the Dublin club and topped the goal-scoring table by May 2005. As the club ran into financial difficulty, mainly due to the costs surrounding the building of Tallaght Stadium, the club was forced to place all their players on the transfer list for free, however this excluded McCourt whom they felt was an indispensable asset of the club. However, after only seven goals in seventeen appearances and following interest from Bristol City and Queen's Park Rangers, Shamrock Rovers, in need of funds, decided to let McCourt go.

The player was signed by his hometown club, Derry City, for a fee thought to be around £60,000. He still ended as Rovers' top goalscorer that season. Paddy McCourt helped Derry City to the runners-up position in both the 2005 and 2006 League of Ireland seasons. He scored six goals in thirty-one appearances for Derry City in the 2007 season and won an FAI League Cup medal. His skill had reportedly interested West Bromwich Albion and Derry City announced in June 2008 that they had reached agreement with the newly promoted Premier League side.

In June 2008, it was reported Derry City had agreed a fee with Celtic with McCourt travelling to Glasgow to finalise terms and undergo a medical at Celtic's training camp in Lennoxtown. West Bromwich Albion had agreed terms with both player and club, but the lure of joining the club he supported as a boy persuaded McCourt to move to Glasgow. On 19 June 2008, Celtic announced that Paddy McCourt had signed for the club for an undisclosed fee after agreeing a three year contract.

William Flood

William 'Willo' Flood was born in Dublin on 10 April 1985. His football career began with the Dublin junior football team Cherry Orchard in Ballyfermot. He moved to England in 2002 when he was signed by Manchester City and made his first-team debut for Manchester City in a UEFA Cup tie against the Welsh team TNS in 2003. A right-sided midfielder with tricky dribbling skills, Flood scored his first goal for Manchester City in a September 2004 League Cup tie against Barnsley, and made a total of twelve appearances in the 2004/05 season. At the start of the 2005/06 season Flood had a three month loan spell at Coventry, but on his return to Manchester City an injury ruled him out for several months. He returned to the fringes of the Manchester City team in March 2006, making a handful of appearances at the end of the season, predominantly as a substitute.

Flood joined Cardiff City in 2006, making twenty-five appearances for them, but seemed to struggle to settle at Ninian Park and was subsequently loaned out to Dundee United for the 2007/08 season. On 15 December 2007 he scored his first goal for Dundee United against St Mirren in a 3–0 win. This goal for Dundee United, his first, earned him the SPL Goal of the Season Award. He returned to Cardiff at the end of season 2007/08. A second season-long loan deal was agreed between both clubs and he returned to Tannadice in July 2008. On 30 January 2009 William 'Willo' Flood signed a two-and-a-half-year contract that took him to his boyhood heroes at Celtic Park.

PLAYERS AND STAFF OF IRISH DESCENT

Paddy Crerand

Patrick Timothy 'Paddy' Crerand was born on 19 February 1939 in Glasgow. He was a Scottish-born footballer of Irish descent. A boyhood Celtic fan from the hoops heartland of the Gorbals, Pat Crerand was a talented attack-minded right half who had the ability to go on to become a Celtic legend.

He signed for the hoops in August 1957 from Duntocher Hibs and made his debut in a 3–1 league victory over Queen of the South at Parkhead on 4 October 1958. Crerand quickly established himself as a key member of the Celtic side and a firm favourite of the support.

A lack of pace didn't prevent him from pushing forward and his ability to deliver defence-splitting balls was second to none. He loved to get forward and shoot from distance. Apart from this willingness to attack Crerand added some real bite to the midfield and he was a player who never shirked a tackle.

However Crerand too frequently lost his discipline on the field and he was at the centre of several disciplinary issues while on international duty with Scotland. Celtic Chairman Robert Kelly clamped down hard on these indiscretions and the relationship between player and chairman was frosty and fragile. During the 1963 Ne'erday game at Ibrox Crerand had a poor first half and subsequently had an explosive half-time row with Sean Fallon.

From that moment his time at Parkhead was all but over. The player asked for a transfer and joined Manchester United on 6 February. Exactly if Crerand was pushed or jumped is unsure and really depends on whose side of the story you believe. One thing for sure is that Crerand's ability on the football pitch was much missed by Celtic.

However, although the player enjoyed significant success in Manchester, he would miss out on Celtic's greatest triumph and, as wonderful as the Manchester United team he played with was, it was less successful than Stein's Celtic.

The common perception is that Celtic remains very close to Crerand but there is no doubt Manchester United is where his heart now lies. Indeed, for all his talk of retaining a 'soft spot' for the Bhoys, Crerand struggles to hide some bitterness towards his former employers. In one interview he admitted that he was in tears when Celtic won the European Cup – not out of joy but because they beat Manchester United to the feat.

He would use his newspaper column to urge Paul McStay to quit Celtic for Old Trafford and more recently in the run up to Celtic's Champions League ties with Manchester United in 2006 he told anyone in the English media who would listen that the Bhoys had no chance against his Red Devils.

In the match programme Crerand also recalls the time he went to see Celtic defeat Manchester United in the Coronation Cup in 1953. He said 'I wasn't supporting United that night, but obviously it will be different for this game'.

This from a man who admitted not seeing a game at Celtic Park for more than twenty-five years. To compound matters, in his match programme column for the Old Trafford tie, Crerand compared 'plucky underdogs' Celtic to non-leaguers Exeter and Burton Albion who had recently played Manchester on FA Cup duty.

Charlie Gallagher

Charlie Gallagher was born on 3 November 1940 in Glasgow to Irish parents from County Donegal. He was the cousin of fellow Celtic player Paddy Crerand. Gallagher first played for St John's (Gorbals) Boys' Guild in 1952, Holyrood Senior Secondary in 1953, before joining Kilmarnock Amateurs in

1955 and Yoker Athletic in 1958. Gallagher was recommended to Celtic by his PE teacher, John Murphy. Murphy had connections with Celtic and doubled as announcer at Parkhead on match days.

On 20 September 1958, Gallagher provisionally signed for Celtic and made his full debut on 6 March 1959. Jock Stein signed him as a full professional on the same day.

Gallagher was part of the Lisbon Lions squad that won the 1967 European Cup final. The same year, Gallagher became the first Scottish-born player to play for the Republic of Ireland when he travelled to Ankara on 22 February 1967 to represent Ireland against Turkey.

Gallagher played for Celtic for over ten years, making a total of 171 appearances and scoring thirty-two goals including 106 Scottish League appearances and seventeen league goals. He also played in thirteen European games.

Gallagher remained at Celtic until 1 May 1970 when he transferred to Dumbarton FC. He retired from playing in April 1973 and worked as a scout for Celtic from April 1976 to April 1978.

Mick McCarthy

Michael Joseph 'Mick' McCarthy was born on 7 February 1959 in Barnsley. He is currently the manager of Wolverhampton Wanderers. He has previously managed Millwall, Sunderland and the Republic of Ireland and has also worked as a television football pundit.

Mick McCarthy made his league debut for then-Fourth Division Barnsley on 20 August 1977 in a 4–0 win over

Rochdale. He spent two years in the basement league, before the club won promotion. Two years later, the team again went up to the (old) Division Two. A strong central defender, he was a virtual ever-present for his hometown club, but departed in December 1983 for fellow Division Two club Manchester City.

The Maine Road club won promotion in McCarthy's first full season and he finally had the chance to play at the highest level. His first season in the top flight was steady enough as the club reached mid-table, but relegation struck the following year. McCarthy himself would not face the drop though, as he moved to Celtic in May 1987.

He picked up his first piece of silverware at Celtic as they won the league and cup double in his first season. The following season McCarthy again won a Scottish Cup winner's medal, although the club had to settle for third place in the league.

McCarthy again moved on to a new country, as he joined Lyon in July 1989. However, things didn't work out for the defender in France and, feeling his international chances were being harmed, he returned to England on loan with top flight Millwall in March 1990. Despite the London side suffering relegation during his loan period, McCarthy impressed enough to earn a move and he was signed permanently in May 1990 for £200,000. His appearances in the next two seasons were often limited by injuries and he effectively retired from playing when he took over as manager of the club in 1992.

Chris Morris

Christopher Morris was born on 24 December 1963 in Newquay, Cornwall. He first began his career in 1982, signing for Sheffield Wednesday under ex-England international and ex-Republic of Ireland manager, Jack Charlton, in the old Division Two. He won promotion to the First Division with Wednesday in 1984. Morris made seventy-four appearances between 1983 and 1987, scoring one goal along the way. He then moved to Celtic, signing for £125,000 on 10 August 1987. He made his debut in the 4–0 win over Morton, at the age of twenty-three. Between 1987 and 1992, Morris was the regular right back for Celtic, with 160 appearances and eight goals to his name. Morris then moved onto Middlesbrough on 14 August 1992, where he remained for several seasons as a first team regular, wowing the fans with top-class defensive displays. He was often in the top three in player of the season votes. Troubled by an anterior cruciate-ligament injury, he retired at the end of the 1996/97 season, when Boro were runners-up in the FA Cup and Football League Cup, but a three point deduction for postponing a match at short notice had caused them to be relegated from the Premier League.

In 1988, Chris Morris caught the attention of Jack Charlton, who by then was the Republic of Ireland boss. Since taking over in 1986, Charlton had begun to make maximum use of the rule that allowed players with Irish heritage to play for the national team. Morris, whose mother, Evelyn, was born in Monaghan, Republic of Ireland, qualified under this ruling. He made a promising debut in the 5–0 friendly win against Israel at Dalymount Park on 10 November 1987. He soon made the number two shirt his own, and played his part in the successful qualification bid for Euro 1988, the Republic's first ever major tournament. Morris played in all three games of the championships, including the famous 1–0 win over England in Stuttgart. He continued in the side that qualified for the World Cup of 1990 in Italy, another major first for the Republic. He played in every game. Ireland failed to qualify for the next European Championships in 1992, and Chris Morris played his final game against Wales on 17 November 1992.

After leaving football Chris went back to Cornwall to work for the family business, Morris Cornish Pasties, which his parents have run since 1971.

Thomas Coyne

Thomas 'Tommy' Coyne was born on 14 November 1962 in Govan, Glasgow. Coyne played for Hillwood Boys Club before starting his professional career at Clydebank, where he made his debut in the 1981/82 season, in which he scored nine goals in thirty-one matches. After scoring nineteen goals in thirty-eight matches in his second season, he began the 1983/84 season with ten goals in eleven games before being sold to Dundee United, then a rising force in Scottish football for £60,000.

However, Coyne failed to reproduce his form at Tannadice and scored only nine goals in sixty-two games, though he did score a few goals in the UEFA Cup. Halfway through the 1986/87 season he was transferred to city rivals Dundee, where he found his scoring boots again, notching up nine goals in twenty games in the second half of the season. In the 1987/88 season Coyne was top scorer in the Premier Division in Scotland as he scored thirty-three goals in forty-three matches. After scoring nine goals in twenty matches at the start of the 1988/89 season, he was sold on to Celtic.

Coyne again failed to reproduce his form at the start of his Celtic career and did not score for the remainder of the season. The following season was also hardly a success, with seven goals in twenty-three games. The next season, 1990/01, saw Coyne revert to his previous form with eighteen goals in twenty-six games, as he finished the season as top scorer. Despite scoring fifteen goals in the following season, and three in ten games at the start of the 1992/93 season, Coyne was transferred to Tranmere Rovers in March 1993.

After a short spell in England, Coyne returned to Scotland to join Motherwell in November 1993 for £125,000. In 1994/95 he was again the Scottish Premier Division's top scorer, and scored fifty-nine goals in 132 games for Motherwell.

Coyne left for Dundee in 1998, where he was loaned out to Falkirk. He then returned to his first club, Clydebank, as player/manager in August 2000 and picked up the Scottish Second Division Manager of the Month award a month later. However, he was sacked after six months after the club had entered administration, despite the club being near the top of Division Two. Soon after leaving Clydebank he joined Albion Rovers where he ended his playing career. His striker son, also named Tommy, signed for Albion Rovers in July 2008 after being released by Dumbarton. After finishing his playing career, Coyne coached Junior club Bellshill Athletic. The club won the West Division One in 2003/04, but Coyne was sacked in July 2005.

In his international career for the Republic of Ireland, Coyne won twenty-two caps and scored six goals. He made his international debut on 25 March 1992 against Switzerland in a friendly played at Lansdowne Road, Dublin. Coyne would have to wait just twenty-seven minutes before scoring his first international goal. He started three of Ireland's four matches in the 1994 World Cup campaign but failed to score in the tournament. His best game for Ireland was the 4–0 victory over Liechtenstein on 12 October 1994, played at Lansdowne Road. Coyne would score two goals in the opening four minutes of the game. He would play his last game for the Republic, coming on as a substitute for David Connolly, in the one-all draw with Belgium on 29 October 1997. This game was the first leg of a play-off for qualification for the 1998 World Cup. Belgium would win the second leg 2–1 and ultimately qualify.

Anthony Cascarino

Anthony 'Tony' Guy Cascarino was born in September 1962 in St Paul's Cray, Orpington, Kent, England. Having originally planned to be a hairdresser and a part-time yoga instructor, Cascarino joined Gillingham FC in 1982 from Crockenhill FC, for a transfer fee of a set of tracksuit tops and some corrugated iron. He went on to play for Millwall, the club he supported as a boy. Millwall had missed an opportunity to sign Cascarino as a youngster and subsequently paid The Gills £225,000 to secure his services. He went on to play for Aston Villa, Celtic in 1991 and Chelsea. However, his most successful years were with Olympique de Marseille and Nancy in the French Ligue Two.

Cascarino was born in England but represented the Republic of Ireland, qualifying through his Irish grandfather. However, he later revealed that his mother told him in 1996 that she was adopted and therefore no blood relative to the grandfather. Cascarino said in his autobiography, 'I didn't qualify for Ireland. I was a fraud. A fake Irishman.' However, through the adoption, his mother gained the right to Irish citizenship and therefore he was indeed eligible.

Cascarino scored nineteen goals in eighty-eight international appearances, making him for a time Ireland's record caps holder. His aerial prowess fitted well with the long ball style of the team. Cascarino was an integral part of the teams that took part in the European Championship in 1988 and World Cups in 1990 and 1994.

Nevertheless, striker Tony Cascarino has to rank among the worst signings in Celtic history. The former Millwall man was signed by the recently appointed Bhoys boss Liam Brady for £1.1 million from Aston Villa in July 1991 (Brady was formerly his agent). At six foot two inches Cascarino was brought to add presence to the hoops forward line but his record of twelve goals in fifty games for the Midlanders was far from impressive.

He made his Celtic debut in a 4–3 victory at Dundee United on 10 August but failed to find the net during a goal fest of a game. Indeed the Celtic support had to wait until 5 October before they saw Cascarino score. That goal came in a game at Hearts and as part of an amazing sequence of events – in a six minute spell the striker came on as sub, scored and was sent off!

He would score the equaliser in a 1–1 draw at Ibrox on 2 November which saved him from being rated our worst ever buy. However, his time at Parkhead would be mercifully brief with the forward complaining Celtic played too much football for his liking! After thirty appearances and a pathetic total of four goals, Cascarino departed Celtic in February 1992 in a great piece of business for the Celts which saw Tommy Boyd head the other way from Chelsea to Celtic.

In his autobiography, Cascarino wrote a chapter on his time at Celtic and was scathing, complaining of the divided nature of football in Glasgow and his frustration. However, on various other occasions he has spoken very well of Celtic, so it is hard to know how he really felt. He fell out with Liam Brady (the then manager) before he left, though his career has been one that only a maverick satirical author could write about. His time at Celtic can be best summed up by the following quote by himself:

If I am honest, I don't think I realised how big the club was. I joined them from Aston Villa, then a pretty big club in England, and I felt as if my career was taking a step backwards. At the time Celtic wallowed in the shadow of Rangers. We were a poor side, barely making an indent into Rangers' supremacy in the league. It was, perhaps, the biggest regret of my career that I was unsuccessful there. I was proud to play for them but, on reflection, I should have stayed and endeavoured to develop. But I wasn't a strong enough personality to be able to cope with the religious bigotry off the field.

Tony Cascarino, 2003

Since retiring from football, Cascarino has become a semi-professional poker player, having appeared in the television series *Celebrity Poker Club* and commentating on the *PartyPoker Poker Den*. He has become something of a cult figure and was referenced in the song 'All Your Kayfabe Friends' by Welsh band Los Campesinos! where the singer tells that 'You asked if I'd be anyone from history/Fact or fiction, dead or alive/I said I'd be Tony Cascarino, circa 1995.'

Aiden McGeady

Aiden McGeady was born on 4 April 1986 in Glasgow. He was tipped as a future football star since he was selected for the Under-Eleven Glasgow Catholic Football School select team at the age of seven. He went to Our Lady of the Missions Primary School and followed on to St Ninian's Secondary School, just a few hundred yards away, in the south side of Glasgow. For a short spell in his young teens, McGeady played for the famous amateur club Queen's Park FC, before the club allowed him to move to the team he supported, Celtic FC.

McGeady went on to captain Glasgow Catholic Schools, and played alongside now Celtic teammate Mark Wilson. He was tracked by many top teams in England and Scotland, with both Alex Ferguson and Liam Brady making personal pleas for the youngster to join Manchester United and Arsenal respectively. He has been described as the most coveted schoolboy footballer in the UK and signed a lucrative boot deal with Adidas at the age of only sixteen.

Aiden McGeady made his Celtic debut as an eighteen-year-old on 25 April 2004, scoring a stunning goal against Hearts in a 1–1 draw in a league match.

An attacking midfield player, McGeady was born in Rutherglen, with his grandparents being from Gweedore. His grandmother, Kitty 'Tim' McGeady, lives in Bunaniver while his late grandfather, Patrick was from Glasagh.

He represented Scotland at a secondary school international tournament in Paris against Brazil, Argentina and England before France 1998 while still at primary school, and officials at the Scottish Schools Football Association (SSFA) were frustrated that later on Celtic wouldn't let the St Ninian's High School pupil play for their Under-Fifteen side, but did eventually allow him to play for an Irish team at the same age level. Both Liam Brady and Pat Bonner had tipped off Brian Kerr, who masterminded their youth set-up before being promoted to managing the full national side, about McGeady's potential and Donegal heritage.

The youngster's sparkling debut centred on that Ronaldinho-style trick. It was a moment which summed up the confidence McGeady displayed throughout his sixty-nine-minute run-out and it led, inevitably, to headlines hailing 'Aideninho'.

He made his full Ireland debut in the close season of 2004, with a substitute appearance against Jamaica in the Unity cup.

Since making his debut, aged eighteen, McGeady has picked up the following awards:

December 2004 – SPL Player of the Month
Season 2004/05 – Celtic Young Player of the Year
November 2005 – SPL Young Player of the Month
Season 2005/06 – Celtic Young Player of the Year
August 2006 – SPL Young Player of the Month

PLAYERS AND STAFF FROM IRELAND AND OF IRISH DESCENT

September 2006 – SPL Young Player of the Month
Season 2006/07 – Celtic Young Player of the Year
Celtic FC Player of the Year 2008
SPFA Players' Player of the Year 2008
SPFA Young Player of the Year 2008
Eircom Republic of Ireland Young Player of the Year 2008

APPENDIX II

CELTIC HISTORICAL FACTS
AND SUPPORTER ASSOCIATION FACTS

CELTIC EMBLEMS

Celtic's first crest was the Celtic Cross, as was seen on the first strip. However, advertisements of Celtic in the early years showed a harp against a blue background. The team also wore a strip with a large shamrock as the badge in the 1950s, and then the strips were without a crest until the late 1970s, when the four-leaf clover became the emblem, which is still used to present day. The Celtic Cross did make an appearance again in the centenary year and in 2003, to celebrate 100 years of the hoops. There was consideration of changing the crest at one short point, but thankfully this was never taken any further. As David McKinney wrote in the *Sunday Times* in October 1994:

> Celtic are preparing to break with years of tradition by changing their club crest. The current image of a four-leaf clover could be replaced or amended as the club attempts to create a new corporate identity. Top-level meetings have taken place as the club's managing director, Fergus McCann,

seeks to make the club more attractive to the Scottish business community. A thistle and the Celtic tartan have already been mooted as possible symbols of Scotland which could be included.

Peter McLean, the club's PR officer, confirmed last night that Celtic are working towards tighter Scottish links.

'We are a Scottish club, and would hope some sort of Scottish element will be incorporated in the new crest. There is a question mark over the two or three different logos currently being used for different purposes and we are looking for one which will fairly depict Celtic Football Club.

There are two or three being considered at the moment, although we haven't yet reached a final decision. We would like a Scottish/Irish image, because we are very proud of our history, and I don't see us moving far away from our traditions.'

The move, however, will anger sections of the club's support who jealously guard Celtic's history and traditions.

The four-leaf clover not a shamrock as many believe, has been part of the club's heritage since they started playing at the present Celtic Park in 1892 and found a four-leaf clover growing on the centre spot before the start of their first game.

There are already signs of disquiet among many of the club's supporters, as they see sentiment making way for a hard-headed American-style business approach under McCann.

A compromise on the crest could be a decision to bring back the Celtic Cross displayed on their jerseys for the centenary year, which proved popular with supporters from Scotland and Ireland.

Supporters might well have the chance to influence the decision. 'We haven't made a final decision yet, and we would consider any suggestions sent in by the supporters,' said McLean.

The story behind the official Celtic crest as seen on the team jerseys and on official club merchandise today has a link back to Ireland in a small but important way. Ned Bradley emigrated from Derry to Glasgow's east end sometime in the 1880s. Ned attended the first Celtic game in 1888 at the original Celtic Park. Among the many immigrant Irish in the east end was a girl named Elizabeth New from Tullamore, Co. Offaly. Ned and Elizabeth were married in Shettleston in 1892 and they produced sixteen children, the youngest, James, was born in 1915.

Along with Charlie Quinn, James co-founded the Bonnybridge Celtic Supporters Club. A member of the club designed the bus plaque that was in time to become the official logo of Celtic Football Club. James was president of the club and one of three delegates of the Celtic Supporters Association.

Both the association members and the Celtic directorate expressed admiration for the Bonnybridge bus plaque. The Celtic directors indicated that they would like to adopt it for their own. After due consultation and consideration, Celtic supporters either at club or association level responded to this 'request' and the plaque design was gifted to Celtic Football Club.

Celtic Football Club in its history has been identified or associated with the following symbols: The Celtic Cross; The Shamrock; The Four-Leaf Clover and the Irish Tricolour Flag.

CELTIC HISTORICAL FACTS AND SUPPORTER ASSOCIATION FACTS

The Celtic Cross

The Celtic Cross is widely used as a Christian symbol, but as we can tell from its name, the cross has a history stretching further back than Christianity. For example, its four arms are interpreted as the four elements (earth, air, fire, water), the four directions of the compass (north, south, east, west) or the four parts of man (mind, soul, heart, body) in various cultures and traditions.

An Irish legend tells how St Patrick created the first Celtic cross by drawing a circle over a Latin cross to incorporate a pagan moon goddess symbol. For an Irish Catholic, the circle in the Celtic cross may be a symbol of eternity and the endlessness of God's love. It can even represent a halo emanating from Christ.

The Christian & Marist Brothers have used the Celtic Cross as their crest.

Celtic, founded by Brother Walfrid, a Marist Brother, had the Celtic Cross as the crest on the first strip. The Celtic Cross made an appearance again in the centenary year shirt and in 2003 to celebrate 100 years of the hoops.

The Shamrock and the Four-Leaf Clover

In Irish tradition the shamrock or three-leaf clover represents the Holy Trinity: one leaf for the Father, one for the Son and one for the Holy Spirit. When a shamrock is found with the fourth leaf, it represents God's Grace.

The mystique of the four-leaf clover continues today, since finding a real four-leaf clover is still a rare occurrence and omen of good luck.

The plants that produce our four-leaf clovers are *Trifolium Repens*, white clover. Although, the plants mainly produce the common three-leaf clover (or shamrock), the 'lucky' four-leaf clovers are not uncommon.

The shamrock became symbolic in other ways as time went on. In the nineteenth century it became a symbol of rebellion and anyone wearing it risked death by hanging. It was this period that spawned the phrase 'the wearin' o' the green'. There is no such thing as a 'shamrock plant'. The word shamrock comes from the Irish word *seamrog* meaning 'little clover'.

Belfast Celtic presented one of the best away strips ever to be worn by Celtic, a white strip, with a green collar and a large green shamrock as the crest. This was worn in the 1950s.

The corner flags at Celtic Park until the 1980s had a shamrock on a white background.

The four-leaf clover has been the main crest of Celtic since the mid 1970s and has appeared on every jersey since that time.

With a four-leaf clover on my breast,
And the green and white upon my chest,
It's such a joy for us to see,
For they play football the Celtic way.

Chorus
It's been ten years, long time indeed,
We stood with pride and we took defeat,
Our beloved team, our ancient ground,
Has been rebuilt, a club reborn.
McCann he rode the winds of change,

And the things he brought will long remain,
A phoenix rising, a house of steel,
And 60,000 Celtic dreams.

[Chorus]

The work is done and the stage is set,
The Celtic dream can now be met,
In a sea of dreams, we're here today,
Let's sit and watch the Champions play.

The Irish Tricolour

The three vertical stripes are a visual reminder of Ireland's political landscape. The Tricolour flag symbolises the two opposing groups in Ireland and the hope of lasting peace between them.

The green represents the Irish, mainly Catholic nationalists and their stand for independence from the United Kingdom. In revolutionary America and France, Liberty Trees were planted to symbolize the establishment of a new society based upon the ideals and aspirations of democracy. Therefore, green is commonly the colour associated with freedom. Green was also the colour the Irish Catholics always used in the flags they rose during their struggles to end English rule over the land.

Orange represents the Protestants of Ireland, or the Loyalists, who remain loyal subjects to the Crown in the United Kingdom. They have also used this colour for centuries, in honour of William of Orange's defeat of Catholic King James II at the

Battle of the Boyne in 1690. After William of Orange defeated King James II, the Protestants dominated most of Ireland for centuries.

Although the Tricolour wasn't adopted as the official flag of the land until after Ireland became a Free State in 1921, the Irish flag as we know it today has been around as a symbol for a long time. It was first unfurled by Thomas F. Meagher, a member of the Young Ireland Movement in 1848.

His own words explain best what the meaning of the colour White is in the flag. It is the hope of every good Irish man and woman that the words of young Mr Meagher will hold true: 'The white in the centre signifies a lasting truce between the "Orange" and the "Green", and I trust that beneath its folds the hands of the Irish Protestant and the Irish Catholic may be clasped in generous and heroic brotherhood.'

Celtic today still flies the Irish Tricolour high over Celtic Park. The most famous incident almost occurred in 1952 when Celtic came within one vote of being expelled from the SFA because it refused to haul down the Irish flag, till then fluttering from the flagpole above the Jungle as a tribute to most of the club's founders but largely neglected and ignored by those attending Celtic Park.

The campaign was led by the long-time secretary of the SFA George Graham, later knighted 'for his services to football'. Desmond White once said, 'He'll roast in Hell for what he tried to do to Celtic.'

Celtic, in the end, was not expelled from Scottish football, thanks to the support of Rangers in the matter.

Belfast Celtic was formed as an imitation of Glasgow Celtic. The teams would play against each other on a regular basis, with Belfast Celtic's ground also called Celtic Park and 'Paradise'. Unfortunately in 1949, they were forced to withdraw from football altogether, due to sectarian elements. They did give Celtic one last gift though, a certain man called Charlie Tully.

Following the demise of Belfast Celtic, the support turned its attention to Glasgow Celtic. This support remains solid to this day, with over 5,500 season-ticket holders who travel to Celtic Park from the Emerald Isle.

Shamrock Rovers in Dublin were formed following the impression made by Belfast Celtic.

Real Betis in Spain wear green and white vertical stripes. This came around when an official of the Spanish club visited Celtic Park in 1902 and was so impressed he took home a set of jerseys back to Seville. Celtic wore the hoops for the first time a year later.

The first team to wear the hoops was a junior outfit called St Anthony's which resided straight across from Ibrox Park!

Why are Celtic called the Bhoys? It is a question often asked. The first time it appeared was on a postcard from the turn of the century which refers to the Celtic team of the time as 'the bould bhoys'. 'Bhoys', however, was a common American slang term for Irish immigrants at least as far back as the late 1840s, so the parallels can be drawn from this.

World famous Irish folk group The Wolfetones have written two songs about Celtic. The first has become a great favourite with the Celtic fans. Called the 'Celtic Symphony', the video for it was actually recorded inside Celtic Park. The second song, named 'Broken Dreams', is more emotional, delving into the darker side of Glasgow and the tragedy that playing for or supporting Celtic can bring.

Celtic strips were famous not only for the 'hoops' but also for the fact they always had the number on the shorts. The tradition ended when regulations in the 1990s forced the club to install numbers on the back of the shirts.

THE YEAR OF THE LISBON LIONS

Jock Stein was born in Burnbank, South Lanarkshire on 5 October 1922. In 1937 he left Greenfield school in Hamilton. After a brief time working in a carpet factory he became a miner and went down the coal pits of Lanarkshire. In 1938 he joined junior football club, Blantyre Victoria. In 1942 he signed for Albion Rovers at Cliftonhill Stadium. He continued working as a miner during the week, while turning out as centre half on a Saturday. Stein made over 200 appearances for the Coatbridge club.

In 1950 Stein became a professional footballer, earning £12 a week with non-league Welsh club, Llanelli Town, but he was desperate to return to Scotland where he had left his wife and young daughter behind. In 1951, on the recommendation of Celtic Reserve team trainer Jimmy Gribben, he was signed by Celtic for £1,200. Stein was signed as a reserve but with injuries to first team players he was elevated to the first team.

He was appointed vice-captain in 1952 and when club captain Sean Fallon broke his arm, the captaincy was passed to Stein. In 1953 he captained Celtic to Coronation Cup success by beating Arsenal 1–0, Manchester United 2–1 and Hibernian 1–0 to become the unofficial champions of Britain. In 1954, Stein captained Celtic to their first League championship since 1938 and first League and Scottish Cup double since 1914. He would remain as captain until the end of his playing career in 1956 when he was forced to retire due to persistent ankle injuries. He had played 148 games for Celtic, scoring two goals, and was given the task of coaching the reserve and youth players.

On 14 March 1960 Stein accepted the managerial position at Dunfermline. He guided them to their first Scottish Cup victory in 1961, beating Celtic 2–0 in a replay. On 1 April 1964 he was appointed the manager of Hibernian and led them to a Summer Cup success. On 9 March 1965 John 'Jock' Stein returned to Celtic Park as the club's first non-Catholic manager.

During the never forgettable season of 1966/67, Celtic won every competition they entered. They won the Glasgow Cup, the Scottish League Cup, the Scottish Cup, the Scottish League Flag and were the first non-Latin team to lift the European Cup. They lost only two games in the entire season.

They won the Scottish Cup in a 2–0 victory against Aberdeen, scoring twenty goals on the way and conceding none in all matches. In the League Cup run, thirty-five goals were scored, including an 8–2 victory against St Mirren. The League Flag was won at Ibrox in front of 76,000 fans with two goals from Jimmy Johnstone. They won the League with three points to spare on second place Rangers. This was the second League title of the 'original' nine in a row.

Celtic's European Cup victory that season could be considered the greatest feat ever by a British team in Europe and paved the way for other British victories. No big money buys were involved; every player was Scottish and every one born within a thirty-mile radius of Celtic Park.

On their way to Lisbon, Celtic beat FC Zurich of Switzerland in the first round, 2–0 in Glasgow and 3–0 in Zurich. In the second round, FC Nantes-Atlantique of France were swept aside easily by a 3–1 victory away followed by the same score in the return leg. Vojvodina Nova Sad of Yugoslavia were overcome by a 2–0 second leg win in Glasgow, reversing a 1–0 defeat in the away leg. In the semi-final, opponents Dukla Prague were trounced 3–1 in the first leg in Glasgow and held to a 0–0 draw in Prague.

The European Cup final was played on 25 May at the Estadio Nacional, in the Portuguese capital, Lisbon. Celtic beat the ultra-defensive and hot favourites Inter Milan 2–1 after trailing 1–0 to a very soft penalty. Tommy Gemmell scored the equaliser with a rocket shot from outside the penalty area and from close in Stevie Chalmers expertly guided another Gemmell shot into the net to score the winner and rewrite the history books.

Jock Stein's Roll of Honour

European Club Champions: 1967

World Club runners-up: 1967

European Club runners-up: 1970

Scottish League Winners: 1966, 1967, 1968, 1969, 1970, 1971, 1972, 1973, 1974, 1977.

Scottish Cup Winners: 1965, 1967, 1968, 1969, 1971, 1972, 1974, 1975, 1977.

Scottish League Cup Winners: 1965, 1966, 1967, 1968, 1969, 1970.

Ronnie Simpson (Goalkeeper), Jim Craig (Right back), Tommy Gemmell (Left wing back), Bobby Murdoch (Right half), Billy McNeill (Captain, Centre half), John Clark (Left half), Jimmy Johnstone (Outside right), Willie Wallace (Inside right), Stevie Chalmers (Centre forward), Bertie Auld (Inside left), Bobby Lennox (Outside left), John Fallon (Substitute goalkeeper, not used).

Jock Stein (Manager), Sean Fallon (Assistant Manager).

In 1975, Stein was badly injured in a car crash (the other car was driving in the wrong direction on a dual carriageway) and, when he returned to Celtic Park, Celtic were not the team they used to be.

In 1978 he became manager of the Scotland international team. Although the team regained some credibility during his tenure, there were no spectacular successes. But Scotland was stunned when Jock Stein died from a heart attack during an international match in Wales on 10 September 1985.

CELTIC'S GREATEST PLAYER

James Connelly Johnstone was born on 30 September 1944 in Bothwell, South Lanarkshire. Nicknamed 'Jinky' for his natural ability to bob and weave past opponents, Johnstone was a member of that glorious team of 1967, the Lisbon Lions. He was voted by Celtic supporters as the greatest ever Celtic player in 2002.

He was spotted by Celtic's chief scout John Higgins and joined the club at the ripe old age of thirteen in 1957 as a ball boy and youth player. He made his first team debut in 1963 and left the Celtic fans in awe and admiration with his dazzling display on the ball. During his career with Celtic, Jinky scored 130 goals in 498 games and won nine League Championships, four Scottish Cups, five Scottish League Cups, and the European Cup. He won only twenty-three full international caps for Scotland during his playing career, scoring four goals. His time with the Scotland squad was often dogged by controversy, usually linked to Jinky's drinking habits.

Jimmy's time at Celtic often had moments of controversy also, with many encounters with Jock Stein. But Jock nonetheless recognised the sheer ability of the 'wee man' with the football at his feet. The di Stefano testimonial against Real Madrid is reputed to be his greatest game in the hoops and di Stefano himself said that Johnstone was one of the best players he had ever seen.

On leaving Celtic in 1975, Jimmy Johnstone had spells with San Jose Earthquakes, Sheffield United, Dundee, Shelbourne and Elgin City but his first love was Celtic and he maintained close relations with the club for the rest of his life.

*

In 2002 Jimmy Johnstone was diagnosed with motor neurone disease. He sadly passed away on 13 March 2006. Many tributes were left at Celtic Park by fans and thousands witnessed the funeral cortege passing through the streets of the east end of Glasgow.

On my first day as Scotland manager I had to call off practice after half an hour, because nobody could get the ball off wee Jimmy Johnstone.

Tommy Docherty (ex-Scotland Manager)

CELTIC HISTORICAL FACTS AND SUPPORTER ASSOCIATION FACTS

My father Jimmy was a scout and coach at Celtic when Jimmy first arrived at Parkhead and told me all about him.

Bob Kelly and Jimmy McGrory both felt he was too small to make the grade but my father convinced them to stick with him and Jimmy would prove them wrong.

I'm sure every Celtic fan is glad my dad made them persevere as he went on to be the best player the club has ever known.

Billy Gribben, London

People might say I will be best remembered for being in charge of the first British club to win the European Cup or leading Celtic to nine league championships in a row, but I would like to be remembered for keeping the wee man, Jimmy Johnstone, in the game five years longer than he might have been. That is my greatest achievement.

Jock Stein

CELTIC HONOURS

EUROPEAN CUP
Champions: 1966/67
Runners-up: 1969/70
Semi-Finalists: 1971/72, 1973/74
Quarter-Finals: 1968/69, 1970/71, 1979/80

UEFA CUP
Finalists: 2002/03
Quarter-Finals: 2003/04

SCOTTISH LEAGUE
Champions: 42 times
1892/93, 1893/94, 1895/96, 1897/98, 1904/05, 1905/06,
1906/07, 1907/08, 1908/09, 1909/10, 1913/14, 1914/15,
1915/16, 1916/17, 1918/19, 1921/22, 1925/26, 1935/36,
1937/38, 1953/54, 1965/66, 1966/67, 1967/68, 1968/69,
1969/70, 1970/71, 1971/72, 1972/73, 1973/74, 1976/77,
1978/79, 1980/81, 1981/82, 1985/86, 1987/88, 1997/97,
2000/01, 2001/02, 2003/04, 2005/06, 2006/07, 2007/08.

SCOTTISH CUP

Winners: 33 times
1893, 1899, 1900, 1904, 1907, 1908, 1911, 1912, 1914, 1923, 1925,
1927, 1931, 1933, 1937, 1951, 1954, 1965, 1967, 1969, 1971, 1972,
1974, 1975, 1977, 1980, 1985, 1988, 1989, 1995, 2001, 2004, 2005.

LEAGUE CUP

Winners: 13 times
1956/57, 1957/58, 1965/66, 1966/67, 167/68, 1968/69, 1969/70,
1974/75, 1982/83, 1997/98, 1999/00, 2000/01, 2005/06.

GLASGOW CUP

Winners: 29 times
1891, 1892, 1895, 1896, 1905, 1906, 1907, 1908, 1910, 1916, 1917,
1920, 1921, 1928, 1929, 1931, 1939, 1941, 1949, 1956, 1962, 1964,
1965, 1967, 1968, 1970, 1975, 1978, 1982.

GLASGOW INTERNATIONAL EXHIBITION CUP

Winners: 1901/02.

NAVY AND ARMY WAR SHIELD FUND

Winners: 1918

EMPIRE CUP

Winners: 1938

VICTORY IN EUROPE CUP
Winners: 1945

ST MUNGO CUP
Winners: 1951

CORONATION CUP
Winners: 1953

CLUB RECORDS

CELTIC GAMES
Victories & defeats
Record victory: 11–0, against Dundee in 1895.

Record victory against Glasgow Rangers: 7–1 in the Scottish League Cup final 1957.

Record victory (Cup final): Celtic 7–1 Rangers, Scottish League Cup final 1957; still British record for the highest score in a domestic cup final.

Record defeat (all): 0–8 against Motherwell in 1937.

Record defeat (home): 0–5 against Hearts in 1895.

Record defeat (post-war home): 1–5 Aberdeen 1947.

Record points earned in a season:

72 (Premier Division, 1987/88, two points for a win);

103 (Scottish Premier League, 2001/02, three points for a win), which is also the SPL points tally record.

CELTIC HISTORICAL FACTS AND SUPPORTER ASSOCIATION FACTS

Attendances

Record attendance (home): 92,000 against Rangers in 1938. A 3–0 victory for Celtic.

Record attendance (Scotland): 146,433; The Scottish Cup final win against Aberdeen FC in 1937 was attended by a crowd of 146,433 (unofficial attendance 147,365) at Hampden Park in Glasgow, which remains a record for a club match in European football.

Record attendance (Europe): Celtic hold the record for the highest attendance for a European club competition match: Celtic v Leeds United in the European Cup semi-final 1970 at Hampden Park, Glasgow. Official attendance 133,961.

Appearances

Record Appearances: Alec McNair, 604 from 1904–25.

Scorers

Most goals in a season: Henrik Larsson, fifty-three.

Record scorer: Jimmy McGrory, 397 (plus thirteen whilst on-loan at Clydebank).

Service

Longest serving player: Alec McNair, twenty-one years 1904–25.

Unbeaten runs

Longest unbeaten run (all): Celtic currently hold the UK record for an unbeaten run in professional football: sixty-two games (forty-nine won, thirteen drawn), from 13 November 1915 until 21 April 1917 – a total of seventeen months and four days in all (they lost at home to Kilmarnock on the last day of the season).

Longest unbeaten run (home): Celtic also hold the SPL record for an unbeaten run of home matches (seventy-seven), spanning from 2001 to 2004 (this run was ended by a 3–2 defeat to Aberdeen on 21 April 2004), and the record for the longest run of consecutive wins in a single season (twenty-five matches).

International Caps

Most Capped Player: eighty, Pat Bonner: Republic of Ireland.
Most Scotland Caps: seventy-six, Paul McStay.

Transfer Fees

Record Transfer fee received: £6,500,000 Stilian Petrov, Aston Villa, 30 August 2006.
Record Transfer fee paid: £6,000,000 Chris Sutton, Chelsea, 11 July 2000.

Europe

Only club in history to have won the European Cup with a team comprised entirely of home-grown talent.

1967, the year Celtic achieved the feat of winning every competition they played.

Hold the record for the highest attendance for a European club competition match: Celtic v Leeds United in European Cup semi-final 1970 at Hampden Park, Glasgow. Official attendance 133,961.

Fastest hat-trick in European Club football: Mark Burchill v Jeunesse Esch of Luxembourg in 2000.

First and only Scottish club to reach the final of the European Cup.

First British club to reach the final and win the European Cup.

First Northern European club to reach the final and win the European Cup.

Four club record European victories:
9–0 KPV Kokkola (Finland), 1970.
8–1 Suduva (Lithuania), 2003.
7–0 Waterford (Rep. Ireland), 1970.
7–0 Valur Rekjavik (Iceland), 1975.

Club record European defeat: 0–5 against Artmedia Bratislava on 27 July 2005.

Celtic Park
13 November 1887 – The newly formed and ambitious Celtic Football Club lease six acres of vacant ground between Janefield Street cemetery and Dalmarnock Street (now Springfield Road) as the site for their new ground. (The site would later become the Barrs factory and is now a new housing development).

8 May 1888 – After months of hard work the new ground is opened with a special challenge game between Edinburgh

Hibernian and Cowlairs. The match is watched by a crowd of 5,000. The new ground has nine admission turnstiles, an open air stand and primitive banked terracing made from earth mounds. The playing surface is 110 yards by sixty-six and is surrounded by a narrow track.

1892 – The club decides to move from its original home after the landlord announces an increase in rent from £50 per year to £500. A former brickyard a short distance across Janefield Street is identified by the club as the location for its new home.

13 August, 1892 – A huge effort sees the brickyard converted into a fine stadium. More than 100,000 cart loads of earth are needed to fill the brickyard's crater but after hundreds of volunteers dedicated weeks of work the new ground boasts a fine playing field, athletic and cycling tracks, a fifteen-tiered stand the length of the Janefield Street side and a fine pavilion. A Celtic Sports event is staged and the ground hailed as an excellent venue.

1895 – Turnstiles are installed at Celtic Park for the first time at a cost of £445. The work is conducted by Lancashire engineering firm W.T. Ellison and Co. which hails the new turnstiles as state of the art.

1897 – Celtic Park stages the World Cycling Championships.

1898 – Director James Grant, with permission from the board, builds a lavish private two-storey stand on the London

Road side of the ground. The luxury stand boasts padded seats and windows which can be shut if it rains. However condensation means the windows are useless and are later removed.

1904 – The 3,500 capacity Janefield Street stand and pavilion are destroyed in a fire. The club purchases the Grant stand from James Grant.

1905 – A covered enclosure is built in place of the destroyed Janefield Street stand.

1914 – The cement cycling track is converted into terracing and Celtic Park's capacity increased to 25,000.

1929 – Another fire destroys the Pavilion. The Grant stand is demolished and the club employs Glasgow firm Duncan and Kerr to construct a new stand which is opened on 10 August when Celtic defeat Hearts 2–1.

1952 – Following safety concerns from Glasgow magistrates, three new passageways are created on the east terracing – the 'Rangers/away' end of the stadium – to allow for easier access and exit.

12 October, 1959 – Celtic's new £40,000 'drenchlight' floodlight system is switched on with the glamour friendly against English champions Wolverhampton Wanderers. Wolves win 2–0.

March 1964 – Celtic announce the launch of Celtic Pools as a means of raising money to pay for team development and ground improvements.

1966 – The Janefield Street enclosure, known commonly as the 'Jungle', is extensively renovated with a new roof and concrete terracing installed.

1968 – The terracing on the east terracing is concreted and covered.

1971 – Major redevelopment work is carried out on the main stand with a new roof, including suspended 100–capacity press box, and extra seats. The new capacity of the stand is 8,686.

1985 – Under-soil heating is installed and new turnstiles are added at the Janefield Street and west terracing parts of the ground.

1986 – The Celtic End (west terracing) is re-roofed with the new structure providing total cover.

1988 – To celebrate the club's centenary year a new facade is built on the main (south) stand. The red brick facade is part of a development which also sees new hospitality and restaurant facilities built along with a new glass-fronted entrance foyer and executive boxes.

August 1991 – Two large electronic scoreboards are erected onto the roofs at each end of the ground.

CELTIC HISTORICAL FACTS AND SUPPORTER ASSOCIATION FACTS

April 1992 – The Celtic Board announces plans to quit Celtic Park and to move to a new £100-million futuristic 52,000 all seater arena in Cambuslang. The plans unsurprisingly, turn out to be empty promises and a desperate smoke-screen created by a discredited board.

June 1993 – A special challenge game is played at Celtic Park to bid farewell to the 'Jungle' which will no longer be a terraced area come the start of the new season.

March 1994 – Fergus McCann assumes control of Celtic and announces the club will stay at its present home which will be redeveloped into a 60,000 all-seater stadium.

1994–95 – Celtic play at Hampden as work begins on the redevelopment of Celtic Park.

5 August 1995 – The new North stand is officially opened by Rod Stewart and the Bhoys return to Celtic Park with a friendly game against Newcastle United.

August 1996 – The Lisbon Lions stand is opened.

August 1998 – The Jock Stein stand is opened and the redevelopment of the stadium is complete.

SUPPORTER ASSOCIATION FACTS

From its very earliest days Celtic has attracted a faithful and vociferous support willing to travel near and far to support their team.

The earliest forms of organised supporters groups sprung up very soon after Celtic's formation and were known as 'Brake Clubs' – so called because of the large horse-drawn wagons they travelled in. These large wagons could hold twenty-five supporters and brakes would make their way from across Glasgow and beyond to Parkhead to cheer on their favourites.

This horse-powered form of transport was suited for getting to matches within the city and in the neighbouring areas of Lanarkshire, Dunbartonshire and Renfrewshire – although for matches further afield the train was really the only viable option. The earliest Brake Club was formed, naturally enough, in the Calton parish of St Mary's in Glasgow's east end, the very place Celtic itself was formed.

This Brake Club and most others were essentially extensions of already established branches of the League of the Cross. The League was a temperance society set up by the Catholic Church. Each parish in Glasgow had a branch and it was from these groups that the Brake Clubs emerged.

In the early days of the club the Brakes would meet at Carlton Place on the south bank of the Clyde in the city centre and close to the traditional Celtic heartlands of the Gorbals. From this point the wagon would travel in a noisy and colourful convoy to the game. Each Brake would proudly display their own unique banner with a picture of a favourite player. As the Brakes grew in number, an annual gathering of the 'United Celtic Brake Clubs' would be held.

It was only natural, given the social climate of the time, that these large groups of mostly working class, Irish Catholic men would contain a political element and it was not unusual to see banners in support of Irish nationalism and trade unions. True to the founding traditions of Celtic, the Brakes also raised substantial money for charity.

With virtually all the Brake Clubs being born from Catholic parishes in Glasgow, it was equally no surprise to find that faith too had a strong influence on the opinions of the members. This was best illustrated in 1897 when the Brakes called for Celtic to ditch its non-discriminatory traditions and field an all-Catholic team. Thankfully the club comprehensively dismissed the idea.

By the 1920s the once thriving Brake Club movement was in an irreversible decline. The emergence of the motorcar and the growth of the railways meant supporters were now finding independent means to attend games. An increased number of alcohol related violence involving Brake Clubs, which had ironically emerged from the temperance movement, also saw membership figures dwindle.

While the Brake Clubs may now be a footnote in the history of Celtic, their legacy is significant and lives on in thousands of supporters clubs found located across the globe today.

The Celtic Supporters Association

The Celtic Supporters Association was the idea of Willie Fanning whose dream became a reality back in September 1944.

These were dark days on and off the pitch with World War II still raging and, in comparison to those horrors, rather more trivially, Celtic was not providing much joy to its supporters and defeat was a regular experience. Indeed, the idea of a supporters association came to twenty-seven-year-old Willie while watching the Bhoys get thrashed 6–2 at Hamilton.

Willie decided to write to the *Daily Record* calling on fellow Celtic fans interested in establishing a supporters club to get in touch. A total of fourteen people replied. Consequently a meeting was arranged at St Mark's and St Paul's Hall, Chester Street in Shettleston. The meeting proved to be a success, a provisional committee was installed and Willie was elected as president.

By the time of the second meeting at the AOH Hall in Alexandra Parade in Townhead, the word had spread. The hall was packed and carloads of supporters from across Glasgow and beyond eager to attend created a traffic jam along the parade.

The Affiliation of Registered Celtic Supporters Clubs

The organisation was the idea of Eddie McCafferty, President of the Greenock Celtic Travel Club and was formed in 1986. Eddie wanted to form the new group because, at that time, supporters clubs could not gain membership of the Celtic Supporters Association and were consequently finding it difficult to get their hands on tickets for the increasing number of all-ticket matches the club was involved in.

Eddie wrote a letter to the *Celtic View* outlining his proposals and the response was overwhelming. At the first meeting of the as yet unnamed affiliation held at The Broomfield Tavern in Provanmill, 300 supporters turned up, as did the then Celtic directors Jack McGinn and Tom Grant. With approval of the Celtic board, a constitution was drawn up and a committee elected and the Affiliation of Registered Celtic Supporters Clubs was given the official seal of approval.

The Association of Irish Celtic Supporters Clubs

The Association was formed in April 1998 as Celtic closed in on finally ending the domestic dominance of Rangers by claiming their first title in a decade. While returning home to Ireland on the ferry, Jim Greenan of the Paul Johnston Celtic Supporters Club in Monaghan and Joe McGrattan of the Eire Go Bragh Celtic Supporters Club in Belfast, decided between them that the time was right to unite all the Celtic Supporters Clubs in Ireland.

The idea behind the AICSC was to finally bring together the many Celtic supporters clubs based throughout the whole of Ireland. Naturally, the idea proved to be a huge success with clubs finally having the opportunity to pool resources and follow the Bhoys with much greater frequency then previously possible.

Delegate meetings are held on a province-by-province rota basis. The association also has its very own successful magazine – *The View from the 32* – which promotes both Celtic and the AICSC. An Annual Charity Dinner is the highlight of the AICSC social calendar and, over the years, the event has welcomed a whole host of past Celtic greats.

The North American Federation of Celtic Supporters Clubs
The North American Federation of Celtic Supporters Clubs
is the umbrella organisation for all Celtic supporters clubs in
the United States and Canada. The history behind the formation of the NAFCSC is one born out of necessity to see Celtic
games live. Celtic supporters clubs were being formed all
across the United States and Canada but there were no live
Celtic games shown so that videos of the games would be
sent from Scotland for viewing.

The Rangers clubs had formed an association and were
getting live games via satellite from time to time, so a collec-
tion of Celtic supporters from Scotland and residing in Canada
decided to act and attempt to get the satellite viewing for
Celtic supporters. Jacky Meehan of the St Catherine's Celtic
Supporters Club, Tommy Donnelly of the Bamalea Celtic
Supporters Club, Harry Aire of the Hamilton Celtic Supporters
Club and Eugene Carney of The Durham Celtic Supporters
Club, all in Ontario, met and decided on what needed to be
done. After a few meetings they initially decided to form the
Canadian Federation of Celtic Supporter Clubs.

Word spread fast of what was happening in Canada and
soon calls came from Celtic supporters clubs in Kearney
New Jersey, Los Angeles, San Francisco, New York, Boston
and Chicago. Within a few days, following a quick meeting,
the organisation founded in Canada was renamed the North
American Federation of Celtic Supporters Clubs. Within four
weeks of its formation, the Federation now had access to
live satellite games of Celtic and boasted a membership of
seventy-two clubs. The Federation hosts a convention in Las
Vegas every second year which 3,000 Celtic supporters attend

regularly to turn the city green and white for the entire week.

With the formation of these Supporters' bodies, the 'Celtic Family' is united wherever it may be. The people of Ireland and its diaspora can claim the identity that is Celtic Football Club as being of Ireland and steeped in the history of Ireland.

NOTES

1 *Hall's Ireland – Mr & Mrs Hall's Tour of 1840* (Sphere 1984)

2 The Cork Heritage Museum, Fitzgerald Park, Mardyke Park, Cork

3 The Wild Geese Heritage Museum, Dominic Street, Portumna, Co. Galway

4 *National Geographic* Vol. 159, No. 4 1981, pp 432-440. 'Ireland – Its Long Travail'. Joseph Judge

5 *Out of Ireland* Dir. Paul and Ellen Casey Wagner (American Focus 1994)

6 The Wild Geese Heritage Museum, Dominic Street, Portumna, Co. Galway

7 *The Celtic Story – A History of Celtic Football Club* James E. Handley (Stanley Paul 1960)

8 *Hanging Crimes* Frank Sweeney (Mercier Press 2005)

9 *The Celtic Story – A History of Celtic Football Club* James E. Handley (Stanley Paul 1960)

10 The Celtic Social Charter. www.celticfc.net/home/corporate/socialCharter.aspx

11 *Sligo Weekender* 1 Nov 2005. 'Sligo to Play Big Part in Celtic Statue Unveiling'

12 *The Celtic Story – A History of Celtic Football Club* James E. Handley (Stanley Paul 1960)

13 *The Irish in Scotland* James E. Handley (Burns 1964)

14 *The Irish in Scotland* James E. Handley (Burns 1964)

15 *Willie Maley – The Man Who Made Celtic* David W. Potter (Tempus 2003)

16 *The Celtic Story – A History of Celtic Football Club* James E. Handley (Stanley Paul 1960)

17 *New Hibernia Review* Vol. 12, No.1 Spring 2008, pp 96-110

18 *Scotland on Sunday* 25 April 2004. Dr Joseph Bradley

19 *Western People* 8 January 2003

20 The Rosses CSC, Donegal. www.rossescsc.com

21 www.belfastceltic.org